Helping your Child to Learn at
# Primary School

LIBRARY
RUGBY COLLEGE

WITHDRAWN

RUGBY COLLEGE OF FE

* 0 0 6 2 9 0 3 1 *

How To Books are designed to help people achieve their goals. They are for everyone wishing to acquire new skills, develop self-reliance, or change their lives for the better. They are accessible, easy to read and easy to act on. Other titles in the series include:

**Achieving Personal Well-Being**
*How to discover and balance your physical and emotional needs*

**Raising the Successful Child**
*How to encourage your child on the road to emotional and learning competence*

**Unlocking Your Potential**
*How to master your mind, life and destiny*

**Successful Single Parenting**
*How to combine bringing up children with your other life goals*

**Thriving on Stress**
*How to manage pressures and transform your life*

The *How To Series* now contains around 250 titles in the following categories:

**Business & Management**

**Computer Basics**

**General Reference**

**Jobs & Careers**

**Living & Working Abroad**

**Personal Finance**

**Self-Development**

**Small Business**

**Student Handbooks**

**Successful Writing**

For full details, please send for a free copy of the latest catalogue to:
**How To Books**
Plymbridge House, Estover Road
Plymouth PL6 7PZ, United Kingdom
Tel: 01752 202301   Fax: 01752 202331
www.howtobooks.co.uk

LIBRARY
RUGBY COLLEGE

# Helping your Child to Learn at

# Primary School

*How to support and improve your child's learning potential*

**POLLY BIRD**

**How To Books**

# Dedication

To the Staff of Grove Vale Primary School

LIBRARY
RUGBY COLLEGE

| ACCESS No. | 629031 |
| CLASS No. | ✓ 372 |
| DATE | ─8 MAY 2000 |

First published in 1999 by
How To Books Ltd., 3 Newtec Place,
Magdalen Road, Oxford OX4 1RE, United Kingdom
Tel: 01865 793806   Fax: 01865 248780
email: info@howtobooks.co.uk
www.howtobooks.co.uk

All rights reserved. No part of this work may be reproduced,
or stored in an information retrieval system (other than for
purposes of review), without the express permission of the
publisher in writing.

© Copyright 1999 Polly Bird

British Library Cataloguing-in-Publication Data
A catalogue record for this book is available from
the British Library

Editing by Alison Wilson
Cover design by Shireen Nathoo Design

Produced for How To Books by Deer Park Productions
Typeset by Euroset, Alresford, Hampshire SO24 9PQ
Printed and bound by The Cromwell Press, Trowbridge, Wiltshire.

NOTE: The material contained in this book is set out in good
faith for general guidance and no liability can be accepted
for loss or expense incurred as a result of relying in particular
circumstances on statements made in the book. The laws
and regulations are complex and liable to change, and readers
should check the current position with the relevant authorities
before making personal arrangements.

# Contents

# List of Illustrations

# Preface

Like many other parents of primary school children you want to help your child with school work. Perhaps you are worried about their lack of progress; maybe you think they are not being stretched enough; or perhaps you simply want to give them a little extra boost.

Your instincts are good – after all, as a parent, you have your child's best interests at heart. The closeness you feel for your child is a good basis for teaching them. But you may be uncertain about where to start. What should you teach your child? And how should you do it?

Reading this book will show you how you can reinforce what the school does. It gives practical ideas for helping your child and explains how to do so positively without undue pressure. It does not forget to tell you how to cope with problems your child might encounter and how to support them within the school's programme.

This book is not intended to replace the teaching programme in your child's classroom. What it does do is give you the confidence and skills to reinforce the work the school does.

Working with your child will enhance your relationship and bring you closer together. You will also find that as you help your child that you discover new interests so that you both become part of the learning process.

*Polly Bird*

LIBRARY
RUGBY COLLEGE
1

---

# Working with the School

The help and support that you give your child should complement, not replace, the work done in school. Your relationship with the school should be:

- based on mutual respect
- cordial
- supportive.

The more you learn about your child's school and methods of teaching the better you can help your child.

## UNDERSTANDING THE NATIONAL CURRICULUM

All schools now arrange their teaching according to the National Curriculum as decided by the government. Understanding it will help you support your child's school work.

The **National Curriculum** is a group of subjects that must be taught to every child between the ages of 5 and 16. The subjects are:

- English
- Maths
- Science
- Design and Technology
- Information Technology (IT)
- History
- Geography
- Music
- Art
- Physical Education (PE)
- a modern foreign language (at secondary school).

Of these subjects three are **Core** subjects and the rest are **Foundation** subjects. The three Core subjects are:

- English
- Maths
- Science.

In Welsh-speaking parts of Wales Welsh is the Core subject rather than English.

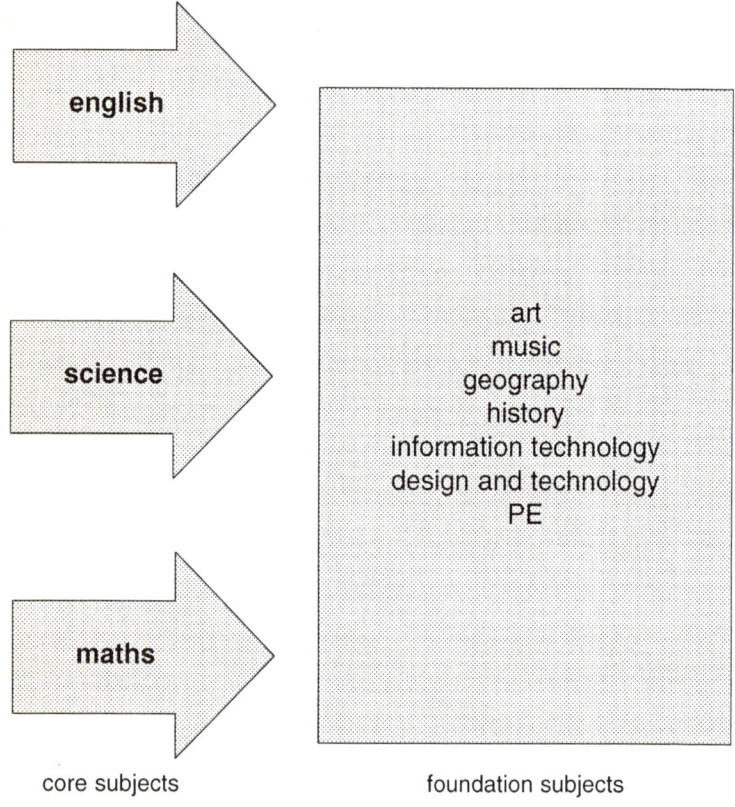

Fig. 1. National Curriculum in the primary school.

In primary school children are taught all the National Curriculum subjects except a modern foreign language. Your child will also have to study religious education (RE). The content of RE is decided locally but must follow the legal guidelines.

Your child's school will decide what the teaching timetable will be and what else to teach the pupils.

## Key stages
The National Curriculum is divided into four stages called **Key Stages**. Each Key Stage is related to pupils' ages as shown:

- Key Stage 1 – ages 5 to 7
- Key Stage 2 – ages 7 to 11
- Key Stage 3 – ages 11 to 14
- Key Stage 4 – ages 14 to 16.

This book deals with Key Stages 1 and 2, that is ages 5 to 11. Every school has documents about the National Curriculum which explain what teachers must teach at each Key Stage.

## Different areas of learning
Most National Curriculum subjects are divided into different areas of learning. For example, English is divided into:

- Speaking and listening
- Reading
- Writing

Schools decide what books and other teaching materials to use. Teachers create their own lesson plans based on the National Curriculum and their pupils' needs.

## Assessment
The National Curriculum sets standards of achievement in each subject for pupils aged 5 to 14. In most subjects these standards range from 1–8. As your children get older and learn more they move higher up the levels. So level 2 standards should challenge 7 year olds while level 4 standards should challenge 11 year olds. More able children reach standards above those that are typical for their age.

Three of the National Curriculum subjects do not have levels 1 to 8. Instead they have a single standard to be reached at the end of each Key Stage. The subjects with one standard are Music, Art and PE.

## Teachers' checks
Your child's teacher will regularly check his or her progress. Teachers also have to assess progress in English, Maths and Science against the

National Curriculum standard when pupils reach the ages of 7, 11 and 14. The teacher decides which level most accurately describes your child's performance in each area of learning in each subject. An overall level for the subject is then worked out.

*Withdrawing your child*
You can withdraw your child from some or all RE (and sex education lessons if the school provides them) but not National Curriculum subjects.

Children with special educational needs may not have to follow all or part of the National Curriculum if it is not suitable for them.

## Children with special needs

If your child has or develops **special needs** your child's head teacher or Local Education Authority (LEA) can arrange for an assessment. You will be informed and consulted about what is happening and when. When the assessment has been done the LEA will prepare a statement describing your child's special needs and giving details about what education should be provided for your child. It will also explain any differences in the National Curriculum that your child should follow.

## CO-OPERATING WITH TEACHERS

Teachers are there to help your child. Most welcome support from parents. Some schools encourage parents to help in classes and this can give a better understanding of what the school is doing.

But remember that teachers have to follow the National Curriculum and to provide certain standards of education. They are professionals who have been trained to do a difficult job and are therefore in the best position to know what and how children should be taught.

But most good teachers encourage parents to support their child's school work. The question is how can you do it without annoying your child's teacher?

You should bear some simple rules in mind:

- Don't start helping your child with school work without asking their teacher first.

- Follow the teacher's suggestions.

- Make sure that the help you give your child complements the school's teaching.

### Asking the teacher first

It is a courtesy and common sense to ask your child's teacher for advice before trying to help them with anything that relates to school work. If you start teaching your child something completely new it might be inappropriate for their abilities, or different from the school's methods or be something which will be taught in class at a later date.

Ask what you can do to help your child and be prepared to alter what you were going to do. If you and the teacher co-operate your child will benefit more.

### Following the teacher's suggestions

Most teachers will have plenty of ideas of ways in which you can help your child with school work at home. It is sensible to follow their suggestions because they will help your child to follow the National Curriculum properly and to take part in activities that are suitable for him or her.

### Complementing the school's teaching

Your child's school may have a particular way of teaching maths or use one particular reading scheme or teach children handwriting in a particular style. It is therefore foolish to try to teach your child completely different methods at home.

Find out from your child's teacher what is being taught and whether there are any special methods or styles that they prefer to use. You can then help your child at home using these methods and you will not confuse the child or annoy the school.


## SUPPORTING HOMEWORK

The government is now keen that all children, including primary school children, do **homework**. It has published guidelines for homework for primary school children.

It suggests that homework for primary children should mainly deal with literacy and numeracy, that is reading, writing, and maths work.

The guidelines stress that help and support from parents and carers is important, particularly for younger children.

*Being good at subjects*
You don't have to be good at subjects to be able to help your child. By supporting the school with homework and taking an interest in what your child does at school you are playing a vital role in helping your child.

## Reading

The guidelines suggest that primary children could read or be read to for between ten and 20 minutes a day. You can help by reading to your child or by reading them a story every day. There is more about helping your child with reading in Chapter 3.

## Number homework

The government guidelines advise schools to set number (maths) homework twice a week. This could involve number games and tasks or more formal exercises for older children that they can do at home. You are expected to help your children with these so do not think that your child will have to struggle with them on their own. The activities set will be suitable for their age and abilities.

Children at Key Stage 2 (aged 7 to 11) might be given more challenging activities to do at the weekends. Your help will be important to give them confidence about doing the activities. You will also find that doing an activity together and making it enjoyable improves your relationship with your child.

## Doing other homework

As well as regular activities involving reading and writing older children might be given other kinds of homework. This will gradually increase in difficulty as they get older. However, it should still be related to their abilities. This homework might involve:

- finding things out

- preparing for school work by reading relevant material beforehand

- preparing to speak about something in class

- more standard written tasks.

*Taking time for homework*
Homework for children at Key Stage 1 (aged 5 to 7) should not take more than ten minutes a day in addition to their reading time. If your child is at Key Stage 2 the other homework time should, gradually, increase until by the age of 11 they are doing about half an hour's homework as well as the time spent on reading activities.

*Homework for children with special educational needs*
If children have special educational needs their homework will be as much like their classmates' as possible. But at the same time it will take account of their needs so that it is set at a level that is not too difficult

or too easy. This needs close co-operation between parents, special needs co-ordinators and class teachers.

*Finding out what your school does*

Many primary schools already have homework programmes that are similar to the guidelines suggested by the government. Other schools do not yet have set programmes but give homework as appropriate. The government hopes that eventually all primary schools will have a homework programme for the whole school along the lines suggested.

Your child's teacher should tell you what the school's homework policy is. If you haven't been told, ask. You could ask if the school would arrange to talk to a group of parents about how they can help their children with homework and what the school would like them to do.

## UNDERSTANDING YOUR CHILD'S NEEDS

It is tempting to want to make your child do much more than he or she is capable of. We all think our children are wonderful, but it won't help them to push them to do inappropriate work. You will spoil your good relationship with your child by pushing them too hard.

You need to understand what kind of help your child needs and to support the school in providing it. Your child might be:

- good at maths, but poor at reading or vice versa
- talented at a practical subject
- shy or nervous
- especially interested in a subject
- needing special help
- needing help with physical skills (*eg* holding a pencil or catching a ball).

As you can see the possibilities are endless.

You should therefore work with your child's teacher to help your child with the things that he or she needs most.

## HELPING WITHOUT PRESSURE

You will not get the best out of a child who is tired, hungry, upset, ill or scared of making you cross. You should not try to make your child do more than he or she is comfortable with. At home do not press them to do more homework than the school has asked for. Nor should you tell your child off if he or she doesn't do work to the standard you think is correct. It is much more important that they enjoy the activity and do their best at it with your support and encouragement.

What you want your child to do is to **enjoy learning** and to be able to look to you for encouragement and support. Try to:

- encourage your child to ask you for help, if necessary
- be generous with praise
- be positive when helping your child to make changes
- spend time with your child on learning activities
- make learning fun.

## SUPPORTING THE SCHOOL

One way you can support your child is by supporting the school he or she attends. Schools need parents who not only care about their child's progress but want to help the school provide the best possible education for all the children. A school which functions well can raise educational standards for everyone. All you need to remember is that ultimately the staff are in charge.

You can support your child's school in a number of ways:

- helping in class
- helping in school
- going on school trips
- attending school meetings
- attending Parents' Association meetings
- helping with fund-raising
- becoming a school governor.

### Helping in class

In some primary schools parents are offered the chance to help informally in the classroom. This will not involve any teaching but might involve such things as setting out paints or listening to children read. If you can help in this way you will free the teacher for teaching tasks and this will benefit all the children including your own child.

Discuss with the teacher when you can help and for how long. You do not have to commit yourself for ever. The only commitment will be to help at a regular time so that the teacher and the children can depend on you. Once you have agreed with the teacher when you will go in the teacher will explain what she would like you to do before each session.

## Helping in the school

Your child's school might also want parents to volunteer for tasks in the school generally. This might include such things as helping to run after school clubs, contributing a particular skill, backstage work for school plays and performances, helping sort out libraries or the contents of cupboards *etc*. There are many cases where an extra pair of hands is useful around a school.

## Going on school trips

School trips are popular with children but take a lot of organising and practical help. If you can spare the time to accompany children on a school trip your presence will be greatly appreciated by the staff concerned.

Trips are tiring for adults and children alike. The adults have to cater for the children's needs. You will be given clear guidance beforehand about which children you will be responsible for, the timing of the day's activities and what the children should be doing, *eg*, completing a worksheet.

## Attending school meetings

When the school asks parents to attend meetings do your best to get there. The subject matter could range from explaining how the school maths or reading schemes work to parents' days when your child's work will be discussed. By attending such meetings you will increase your knowledge of the way the school works and also of what progress your child is making. It will also help you understand why your child is working in a certain way. You will also be demonstrating your support for both your child and the school.

## Attending Parents' Association meetings

Most schools have an association for parents whether called a Parent Teachers Association or Friends of the School. It is a chance for parents to discuss issues that concern them and to communicate with the staff in a friendly way. By attending meetings of the group where possible you will be able to contribute your opinions and to learn what is going on in the school. It is also a good way to get to know other parents.

## Helping with fund-raising

You might groan at the thought of helping with school fund-raising but it is important to schools which are often stretched for money. Extra funds might pay for much needed equipment or for special trips.

Fund-raising can take many forms – raffles, fêtes, cake sales *etc* – but if you can help it will make things go better. If you can contribute money, fine; if not offer your services to help with a stall or sell raffle tickets.

## Becoming a school governor

If you have the time and commitment you might consider becoming a school governor and taking part in making decisions of importance to the school as a whole. Governors are elected so you will have a chance to stand. If elected you will be expected to attend at least one meeting a term. It is a good way of taking an active part in supporting the school and helping to implement changes.

## DISCUSSING YOUR CHILD WITH STAFF

There may be a time when you feel that you need to discuss your child with their teacher or even the head teacher. This can be a frightening prospect for many parents. Teachers and head teachers can seem awesome and as professionals you might feel that their word is more important than yours. You need to remember two things:

1. You know your child better than anyone else.

2. Your opinions about your child are just as important as the teacher's.

That doesn't mean that it is a good idea to go in and be aggressive and antagonistic. Such an attitude will make discussion difficult, especially if the subject is likely to be a tricky one. Go in with the attitude that the teacher has your child's best interests at heart and that co-operation is the best way forward.

### Discovering your child's point of view

If you decide to see the teacher make sure that it is because you really need to. Also find out what your child thinks. You should tell your child if you are going to talk to their teacher. You need to reassure them that you're not going to make things worse or embarrass them. In some cases your child may prefer you to let them deal with a problem themselves. Let them try to do this if they want to but be ready to take it to the teacher if their efforts fail.

Try to see a problem from your child's point of view. Decide whether the problem is one that your child has expressed concern about or one that *you* think is important.

### Don't be hasty

If your child mentions a problem do not immediately rush off to see their teacher. For instance, if they tell you that they have been told off for talking in class you need to explain that it may seem hard but that talking in class is not allowed at certain times because it is important to hear what the teacher has to say. Your child has to learn to obey the class rules for the sake of the other children as well as themselves.

## Meeting with a teacher

Remember that the keys to a good discussion with a teacher are:

- make an appointment

- preparation

- politeness

- persistence

- co-operation.

### Making an appointment

When it is important to see the teacher make an appointment. Teachers are busy people and only very simple problems can be solved by a few informal words at the end of the day.

### Preparation

You should prepare for any meeting with a teacher by writing notes about what you want to talk about and questions you want to ask. That way you will not waste time.

### Politeness

You will not get anywhere by being rude and aggressive. The teacher will simply become angry and defensive and no sensible discussion will take place.

Keep calm, make your points and ask your questions calmly and allow time for the teacher to reply. Listen carefully to what they have to say.

*Persistence*

Although you should remain calm and polite do not be deterred from finding out what you want to know. Use polite but firm follow up questions to any answers you get that do not seem to answer your concerns. For example:

● I understand that but perhaps you would explain the last point further.

● You don't seem to have mentioned .... Please could you explain ....

● I understand that as far as it goes but it still doesn't answer my question about .... I wonder if you would tell me what the policy is on that?

Remember that a discussion with a teacher or head teacher will be of no value unless you get the answers to the questions you want to ask or can discuss your concerns.

But in return you should play fair by keeping to the concerns you have and not adding extra general discussion. Neither you nor the teacher has time to waste.

*Co-operation*

You are aiming for what is known in business as a win-win situation. That is, both you and the teacher should end the discussion feeling that you have fairly expressed your point of view and that the outcome is satisfactory to everyone.

The best way forward is through co-operation. Even if there are some points that you do not agree on try to find things that you can both act on. So for example, you may be concerned about your child's reading progress. You don't agree with the way the reading scheme is operated. But you and the teacher agree that you can borrow some extra books to help your child with reading at home.

Finally, leave on a positive note. Don't forget to say thank you and smile. Teachers work hard and often feel unappreciated nowadays. A little praise will go a long way to cementing friendly relations.

## QUESTIONS AND ANSWERS

*Do I have to be clever to help my child?*

Don't worry – you don't have to be super-intelligent to help your child. The best help you can give is to be supportive and interested in what he or she does at school. You will find that as you and your child tackle activities together that you know more than you realise. Also you will both learn new things together.

*My child's teacher wants me to help in class. Will I be expected to teach anything?*
The teacher is in charge of the class and the way subjects are taught. You will not have to teach but you might be asked to share your skills, for example, by showing children to do some simple cooking. You will be asked to do things well within your capabilities like hearing children read.

*Will my child do better if I give him or her extra homework?*
Do not make your child do more homework than the school has asked. At primary school age the important thing is to make sure that your child completes the homework given and gets into the habit of doing it. It will be suitable for your child's capabilities. If you try to make your child do lots of extra homework he or she will become tired and you might put them off. However, if your child asks to follow up some homework of their own accord that is all right. But don't let them overdo it.

## CASE STUDIES

### Sally struggles to support Geoff

Sally is 32 and a single mum. She lives in an inner city tower block and has a part-time job as a secretary with a local building firm. Her son, Geoff, is 5 and is in the reception class of the local primary school. Sally likes the supportive atmosphere of the school but is worried, because there are so many children needing a lot of help, that Geoff will fall behind. He is a bright boy and she wants to help him. She has two free days a week and has decided to talk to Geoff's teacher to see how she can help him at home.

### Robert and Mary are keen to help Becky

Robert and Mary live in the pleasant suburb of a country town. They both work and their 7-year-old daughter Becky is collected from school each day by a local child minder. Both parents try to spend time with her in the evening. The local primary school is modern and children come quite long distances to attend it. The head teacher is keen on computers and new technology and has just ordered a computer for every class. Becky is a very shy girl and her parents discover that she is not getting to use the computer much because her class partner does all the work. They want to encourage her to become more outgoing and at the same time give her more opportunity to become familiar with computers.

## Harry is a house husband

Harry's wife, Jenny, has a good job as a manager at a large store. Harry has just been made redundant and so is making the most of being a house husband and available to support their children Eddy and Mark. Eddy is in year two and loving every minute. He has made friends and his work is excellent. In fact his teachers and parents think he needs to be stretched more so Harry is going to try to help him at home. Mark, two years older, is less able but is keen on sport and has a particular aptitude for gymnastics. Eddy wants to encourage him with the sport but without pressuring him. At the same time he would like to help Mark with the rest of his school work. He has to try to help both his sons without making one jealous.

## SUMMARY

- Understand how the National Curriculum works.

- Co-operate with your child's teacher and the school.

- Help your child to do any homework set.

- Don't push your child too hard – understand what your child needs.

- If your child has special needs discuss them with the school.

# 2

## Supporting Your Child's Learning

Your child will achieve most at primary school by your continued support. Your encouragement will enable him or her to do well and bring you closer together. Your child will feel loved and cared for as you spend time with each other.

But before you start helping your child with school work you need to solve any other problems first. A child who is unhappy, uncoordinated, desperately shy or who has a physical or other kind of problem will not be able to work well. So before you start to encourage your child to do more you need to ensure that he or she can cope with what the school offers now.

### DEALING WITH PROBLEMS FIRST

There are several kinds of problems that you should look out for and which should be dealt with to enable your child to achieve his or her full potential at school. Some of them may be hard to spot; others might be obvious. They might include:

- poor eyesight

- hearing problems

- other physical disabilities

- special needs

- lack of concentration

- dyslexia

- being a gifted child

- having general heath problems.

Where problems are severe enough to need special help and/or different versions of the lessons then they are called special needs.

## Poor eyesight or hearing

If your child seems to miss much of what goes on in class it might be due to poor eyesight or hearing. It is possible for this to be missed as children can become adept at finding ways around the problem.

First ensure that your child attends any school eyesight and hearing tests. These tests often pick up any problems. If between tests you notice hearing or sight problems get your child checked by your doctor.

Once either eyesight or hearing problems have been corrected you should inform the child's teacher so that they can keep an eye on your child and ensure that they are placed where they are best able to see and hear.

*Checking eyesight*

Whether or not your child gets regular eyesight checks at school you should ensure that you take him or her to your doctor or an optician immediately if you suspect that there is an eyesight problem.

Young children do not enjoy wearing glasses but can be encouraged to do so if they are allowed to choose the frames. There is some financial help for buying glasses for children under 16. It is important to get eyesight corrected as soon as possible because early help can prevent more severe eyesight problems later on.

*Checking hearing*

Hearing problems can be tricky to diagnose because they are not necessarily simply complete loss of hearing. A child might hear sounds only at a certain pitch or from a certain direction, for example. Children can also be adept at compensating by asking friends what was said or watching what others do.

If you or the teacher suspect that your child has difficulty hearing your first stop should be the doctor. The problem could be something as simple as ears blocked by wax, which can be dealt with simply. If the problem seems more severe your child will be given an appointment at the local hospital for tests. The result might be a hearing aid or even a minor operation.

Again it is important that hearing problems are dealt with as soon as possible because lack of hearing can severely hamper a child's learning ability.

## Other physical disabilities

Your child may have other physical disabilities which impede movement. If this is the case he or she will already be receiving care from your doctor. Schools go to great lengths to ensure that children with physical disabilities can take part in as much of the school activities as possible.

Other children may tease your child but on the whole children are very supportive of others in need of special help.

If your child needs special equipment or a helper discuss it with the school so that they can do their best to accommodate your child.

## Special needs

Whether your child can cope in a mainstream school will depend on the nature of your child's needs and the result of their assessment by the LEA. The tendency now is to try to accommodate all children unless the disability is too severe. Sometimes this is in a class with special needs teachers.

You will undoubtedly already have discussed your child's needs with the school. But you can help by ensuring that the school is kept up to date with any changes in your child's needs. Your support with school activities and homework is especially important if your child is to get the most from school.

## Dyslexia

Dyslexia is a specific learning difficulty and should only be considered after hearing, eyesight, teaching problems or a general learning disability have been ruled out. Dyslexia is an inability to make sense of the written word although the child might be highly intelligent.

If your child has reading or spelling problems do not assume that they are lazy or bored but also do not immediately assume that they have dyslexia. If problems persist enlist the school's help in getting your child tested by a specialist in dyslexia. If the problem is diagnosed help can be given that will greatly improve your child's ability to read and write. Specific advice can be obtained from the British Dyslexia Association (see Useful Addresses).

## Being a gifted child

You might not think that being a gifted child would be a problem but for many gifted children it is. A gifted child might become bored, disruptive, withdrawn, miserable and be bullied for being different.

Sometimes a gifted child is mistaken for a lazy one because they do not bother with work that seems to them simple or boring. It is important that you discover if your child is gifted if he or she seems lazy – or is simply lazy!

Not all primary schools are able to cope with gifted children. If you think your child is gifted your child's teacher will probably already have noticed this. The problem comes in deciding what to do about it.

Generally asking the school to move your child out of his or her class and away from the peer group is ill advised because it will isolate your child from his or her friends and group experiences. However, the school may have difficulty in providing extra, more appropriate, work.

You can help your gifted child by encouraging out of school activities that would interest and stretch them more. The National Association for Gifted Children (NAGC) can give you advice about supporting your child (see Useful Addresses).

## Dealing with general health problems

At primary school age general health problems are usually minor but should be dealt with. These might include:

- dental problems

- obesity

- cleanliness.

These will not in themselves hinder your child's learning but might make them the butt of bullying. An unhappy child cannot work well.

*Dental problems*
Poorly maintained teeth can be painful and unpleasant to look at. They can also cause bad breath and lead to many painful fillings or even extractions.

Regular dental checks are vital. Even if your child is seen by the school dental nurse this is not enough to counteract a problem. At primary school age your child should see a dentist every four months. Not only can any problems be dealt with before they get worse but your child will get advice on general dental care such as the correct way to brush teeth and gums. Bad breath can be a dental problem and can also be dealt with. If more serious problems are discovered early correction by either the dentist or the doctor will alleviate them.

You can help your child by:

- discouraging sweets or sugary drinks between meals

- making regular dental appointments

- ensuring teeth are brushed correctly and regularly.

*Obesity*
Being overweight not only endangers your child's health but also makes

him or her the butt of other children's cruelty. The picture of the fat child tormented by classmates is unfortunately a reality rather than myth.

There is a lot of advice available about healthy eating. Your doctor or health visitor can give you up-to-date information. A seriously overweight child should be taken to the doctor for advice on how to reduce your child's weight.

You should do your best to ensure that your child eats more greens and fibre than biscuits and chips and takes exercise. You can help by:

● providing fruit, vegetables and fibre

● discouraging snacking

● encouraging exercise – perhaps something you could do together or a sport like swimming.

## PRACTISING PHYSICAL SKILLS

There are a number of simple physical skills that will help your child do well at school. Many young children are naturally uncoordinated and others simply have not had enough practice at simple skills. Skills that your child will need include:

● using scissors

● holding a pen/pencil/paintbrush

● throwing and catching a ball

● tying shoelaces

● doing up buttons

● running, jumping, climbing.

Children don't necessarily learn physical skills by picking them up as they go along. Like most people children learn more quickly if they are shown how to do something.

You will need to teach your child to tie shoelaces and do up buttons. You can also play simple ball games to help them practise throwing and catching. Playing football, running races together, can help with physical co-ordination. This is not only healthy but fun for both of you!

Skills such as using scissors or holding a pencil need to be taught – even how to blow bubbles with a bubble holder! Show your child how to do it and then help them to copy you while you both cut, draw or blow bubbles! Don't be afraid of teaching your child motor skills.

## QUESTIONS AND ANSWERS

*How can I help my child become more co-ordinated?*
Make learning physical skills fun. Repetition and praise is the key. Show your child how to do things correctly, for example, the correct way to use scissors, or how to catch a ball with both hands. Play games or other interesting activities using these skills.

*Should I teach my child to spell?*
Spelling can be difficult for many people, even adults! Provide lots of opportunities to read. The more your child reads and the greater variety of the reading matter the sooner he or she will recognise the correct spelling of words. Occasionally point out incorrect spellings but don't constantly criticise.

*My child doesn't like taking exercise. How can I keep her healthy?*
Your child will do PE and swimming at primary school, but may not like exercise outside. Find activities that she does enjoy but that she might not realise are exercise, for example, dancing to pop music or roller blading. You could join in too!

## ENCOURAGING IMPROVED CONCENTRATION

Some children are unable to concentrate for more than a few minutes at a time. Usually this is simply a lack of practice and habit. In some children the problem is severe enough to be a medical condition called **Attention Deficit Disorder** (ADD).

Learning to concentrate is very important. Not only does your child need to be able to stick to a task in order to learn better but also because a teacher cannot hope to teach in a satisfactory manner if the class is disrupted constantly.

*Helping your child to concentrate*
If your child simply needs practice in sitting still and concentrating this is something you can help with at home. Insist that your child listens for a certain number of minutes or sticks to a task until it is finished to foster a habit of concentration.

If your child has ADD then you should ask your doctor what help is available. You can also contact the ADD Information Service (see Useful Addresses).

*Helping your child focus*
Use simple sentences to help your child focus on what he or she needs to do. For example, you could say:

- Eddy, listen to me. I'm going to tell you where to put your toys.

- Anne, look at this page and read it to me from the top.

- Jack, watch how I do this. Then you're going to do it.

*Asking for explanations*
By asking your child to explain or describe something that has just happened you reinforce understanding and concentration by repetition. 'Let's see if you can remember what I told you about the film we're going to see.'

*Improving attention by praising*
Reinforce improved concentration by praising your child. 'You listened to that carefully. Well done!' But don't be afraid to ask for repetition of an action if your child has still not concentrated properly.

*Other ideas to help your child concentrate*

- Allow TV for short periods but insist that the child watches all of it. Gradually increase the time allowed.

- Listen to the radio or tapes together. Insist they sit with you and listen for a certain length of time – perhaps ten minutes. Ask questions about what you heard afterwards. Gradually increase the time.

- Play a board game and insist that once you start you finish.

- Allow your child to play on the computer but only if they finish the game they start.

Give rewards for concentration – perhaps a trip to the park if your child listens to a tape for 15 minutes.


## LISTENING TO YOUR CHILD

One of the most important ways you can help your child is by listening to them. You might think that you already do that. But think back. How often have you said 'In a minute' when your child has tried to speak to you or 'Not just now' or 'Later, I'm busy'? Nine times out of ten you have then forgotten that your child wanted your attention.

Listening to your child is not just a duty, it should be a pleasure. It is also an important part of supporting your child's learning. Your child needs to know that you are interested in what they do and what they think. You need to listen carefully enough to be able to help them with school work and to hear when there are problems. Many children try to cope with problems at school on their own because nobody has listened to them.

Listening to your child will:

- show them you care

- show them you are interested in them

- help you spot problems

- enable you to help them

- show you what they are interested in

- encourage togetherness.

## Showing them you care

To listen properly to someone involves concentration. By concentrating on what your child is saying you show them that you are genuinely interested in them and what they have to say. Listening properly means 'active' listening, something that not everyone does.

*Listening actively*
You listen actively by:

- looking at your child

- making 'interested' noises and gestures *eg* yes, good, nodding

- making affirmative comments *eg* 'so you think that...'

- asking interested questions *eg* 'That sounds difficult. So what did you do then?'

## Showing your interest

Good listening shows that not only do you care about your child but you are interested in what they have done or think. A child who feels that his or her opinions and activities are valuable and interesting grows in confidence.

### Spotting problems

One of the most important things that happens when you listen to your child is that you are able to spot problems. These problems may not be stated outright, for example, your child might not tell you directly about being bullied or finding the work too hard. But problems will emerge as you listen to your child – perhaps by a different tone of voice or even silence when certain things are mentioned.

By listening carefully you can often spot problems which you can then ask your child about gently. The sooner problems can be dealt with the happier your child will be.

### Finding out what interests your child

Listening to your child will give you an idea about what they are particularly interested in. You can then show interest in this and plan activities that they would enjoy. It is a chance to become closer to your child as you begin to share the things that they care about.

## PRAISING AND CRITICISING CONSTRUCTIVELY

We all want to tell our children that they are doing well. At the same time we need to be able to criticise when they do something wrong. The difficult part is finding the right balance between fairness and overreaction.

### Praising your child

A child who feels encouraged and that they have done well enjoys learning and wants to improve. Encouragement is always a good thing. However, as your child gets older they will themselves become wary of unstinting praise as they become more discerning.

Praise should always be positive. Don't devalue it by making remarks like 'for a child your age' or 'but your brother Ben did a better one' or the damningly uninterested 'that's nice dear'.

Try to refer to specific points *eg* 'That's a lovely colour on that house' or 'that story you've written is very exciting'. This is particularly important when it is rather bad so you need to find something positive.

Modern studies have shown that children who are praised for how hard they have worked or how well they have tackled a difficult task do better than those who are told how clever they are.

### Criticising constructively

In order to help your child you need to point out to them where they have gone wrong or not done so well. It is hard for parents who want to encourage their children. But ignoring mistakes won't help your child in the long run.

Small mistakes can be safely ignored. It is not going to harm your child if a word is spelt wrongly or a story has been written on the wrong page. Nor should you judge creative work by adult terms. The sky may not be green, nor a cat have seven legs, nor the lady in the spotted dress look like you. But the greatest artists have reinterpreted the world and this is your child's vision of it. But, for example, if they consistently get subtraction sums wrong or have misunderstood a basic concept in science then they need to be corrected.

*Knowing how to criticise*
To criticise a child you need to start with the positive. So first find something good to say, for example, 'You have worked very hard at those sums, David'. Then lead gently into helping 'It looks as is you've been having problems with some of the sums. Shall we see if we can work them out together?' Using this approach you will encourage your child but at the same time help them.

## CASE STUDIES

### Sally takes Geoff to the optician

Geoff's teacher contacts Sally to say that Geoff seems to be screwing up his eyes a lot and has started trying to sit next to the blackboard as often as possible. 'He always seems to be talking to the child next to him. I think he's asking what I've written.' She thinks he might have eyesight problems. Sally takes Geoff to the optician who diagnoses short sight and astigmatism. Geoff needs to wear glasses to correct these problems. He is unhappy about it but Sally points out that his best friend John wears glasses and also lets him choose the frames. Geoff quickly gets used to wearing glasses and now sits with his friends near the back of the class.

### Mary and Robert listen to Becky

One day Becky comes back from school but does not go and play with her new rabbit. She seems quieter than usual and rather glum. The child minder mentions this to Robert when he gets home. Robert always tries to spend some time with Becky as soon as he gets in from work and listens about her day. This time Becky doesn't want to say much. Robert gently asks her about her day. Eventually Becky mentions that a bigger boy Toby has been chasing her at break so she can't play with her friend. Robert listens carefully and promises to see what he can do. He speaks to the child's teacher and the boy is quietly warned to leave Becky alone. The next day Becky can't stop talking about her new friend Emma.

### Harry helps Mark concentrate

Unlike Eddy, Mark prefers to be doing sport rather than sitting still reading or writing. In fact he often finds it hard to concentrate or sit still for long. Harry realises that Mark will not do well in school if he does not learn to concentrate more. He starts to insist that Mark completes a few simple tasks each evening before going out to play football with his friends. He knows that Mark finds it difficult to concentrate so he sits with him while he completes homework or watches TV. As a reward for concentrating he lets Mark stay out an extra ten minutes with his friends.

### SUMMARY

- Deal with problems first.

- Don't neglect general health problems.

- Help your child practise physical skills.

- Encourage your child to concentrate on tasks.

- Take time to listen to your child.

- Praise generously and criticise constructively.

# 3

## Improving Language Skills

Good language skills are the basis of improved attainment in all subjects. Without the ability to read, write, speak and listen effectively children cannot achieve their potential at school. Even subjects such as maths require good reading and writing skills for reading and understanding mathematical problems and writing explanations of the answers.

The National Curriculum divides language skills into three areas:

1. speaking and listening

2. reading

3. writing.

Your child's school will provide the basis of learning these skills and stimulation to practise and improve them. But it is important that you help your child to reinforce these skills at home.

### ENCOURAGING SPEAKING AND LISTENING

Children need to be able to express themselves clearly and logically. They also need to be able to concentrate on and understand what is being said to them. Both these skills are important if children are to make the most of primary education. Success in these skills enables your child to:

- absorb spoken information and instructions

- understand spoken arguments

- concentrate long enough to complete a task.

#### Speaking
The ability to explain and describe so that other people understand what is meant is important for all children.

Children can practise speaking by:

- telling stories
- discussing ideas
- describing events, observations *etc*
- reading aloud
- presenting their work to an audience *eg* through drama.

*Helping your child to speak*
There are several ways that you can help your child's speech:

- read poems and stories together
- ask your child to tell you a story
- ask your child to describe a favourite toy or trip
- ask your child to explain how they did something
- discourage unnecessary repeated words such as 'like'.

*Reading together*
By reading a poem or story aloud and then asking your child to read it aloud with you, you are encouraging clarity of speech and practising the natural rhythms of speech. Nursery rhymes and nonsense songs are good for this. Try some of the modern poetry books for children (see Further Reading).

*Your child tells you a story*
It doesn't matter whether the story is made up or one that you have told them. By telling the story again to you your child is practising speaking clearly and making sense.

*Describing a favourite toy or trip*
Description is important because it is the basis of a lot of speech – describing something that happened or an object. By asking your child to describe something to you in speech you are asking him or her to order their thoughts logically and clearly.

*Explaining how something was done*
If your child can learn to explain clearly how they did something – for example set the table, tie shoelaces or build a house with building bricks – they are learning to communicate clearly. Ask questions such as 'What did you do first? Then what happened?' to help your child describe things in the right order.

*Discouraging repeated unnecessary words*
However your child speaks to friends you should discourage the use of unnecessary repeated words such as 'like' or 'you know'. Not only does it sound lazy but it makes your child's speech less understandable. It also tends to encourage rambling speech because of lack of concentration.

*Using different language at home and at school*
Your child's accent is not important. What is important is that he or she is able to speak clearly and be understood. Do not worry if your child speaks one way at home, another at school and yet another when playing with friends. Most people tend to adapt their speech according to the circumstances. You can help by making your child aware of the proper speech patterns for different circumstances so that they do not use the speech of the playground in class or home, for example.

## Listening

Some parents and teachers are concerned that many primary children do not have the ability to sit still and listen to stories or explanations. They are used to watching television and being able to get up and wander off during programmes when they want to. So their concentration span is short. This means that they:

- misunderstand spoken instructions

- do not remember what was said to them

- cannot complete a task.

*How you can help*
Start by insisting gently that your child finishes watching any television programme that they start. Say 'You have started this so you must finish it'. Try to ensure that your child watches interesting programmes.

*Listening games*
With younger children try making a tape recording of different kinds of sounds, *eg* animal noises, noises around the home such as a vacuum cleaner, *etc*. Play the noises one at a time and see if they can guess what they are. Older children can listen to stories on tapes either with or without a book to follow (see also Chapter 2).

## REINFORCING READING SKILLS

The ability to read well is one of the most important skills your child will learn. At the same time it is one that seems to worry parents more than anything else at primary school age.

Your child will learn to read:

- a wide range of literature suitable for his or her age

- for information.

He or she will learn:

- to recognise pattern and rhyme

- grammar

- phonics and phonic patterns (language sounds).

Do not compare your child's reading ability with other children's but with their own progress. Every child will learn to read at a different rate and a different age.

You can help your child with reading first and foremost by not getting worried about it. If you overreact you will upset your child and might put them off reading for a long time. Learning to read should be fun.

Remember to contact your child's teacher to find out what reading scheme, if any, is in use and what books the teacher would prefer you to use at home.

The most important ways to help your child with reading are:

- check that your child holds the book the right way up

- show your child how to follow words from left to right, top to bottom

- read to your child every day for ten to 20 minutes

- listen to your child read every day for ten to 20 minutes

- play word games.

*Holding the book the right way*
For younger children simply learning how to handle a book is an important aspect of learning to read. Once they understand which way up books go they can start to recognise the correct shapes of words and letters.

*Following words with a finger*
Use your finger, or ask your child to use a finger, to show your child how to follow words in a book from left to right, word to word, line to line, top to bottom, left page to right page. This does several things. First it reinforces the way that we in the western world read. Next it allows your child to reinforce the sequence of words. It also encourages your child to look at each word as their finger arrives under it. By following words with a finger either as *you* read them, or as your child either 'tells' the story on her own, or reads it herself, she will begin to anticipate what word is likely to come next in a sentence and start to recognise individual words. As your child's reading improves he or she will use a finger less frequently.

*Reading to your child*
This is recommended as part of homework and the amount of time suggested is ten to 20 minutes. This is long enough to be pleasurable and useful but not enough to bore your child. If you are unsure about the kind of books to read, your child's teacher or the librarian in the children's section of your local library will be able to recommend some.

*Hearing your child read*
Whatever stage in reading your child is at, it is important that you should hear them read. Again this should be part of the time allowed by the National Curriculum recommendations. If your child is just beginning, read the story to them and then ask them to 'read' it to you while running your finger under the words. Older children can read a few pages of a book to you themselves. Don't ask for more than a few pages – that is quite enough for concentration each day.

*Playing word games with younger children*

1.  **Fishing:** make some letter cards and stick a paper clip on each one. Make a fishing rod with a magnet on the end. Your child hooks a card and then has to say a word starting with the letter. If he gets it right he keeps the card; if not it gets put back.

2.  **Flashcards:** make a set of object picture cards and a set of cards with the matching name of the object on them. Ask your child to choose a picture then match it to the correct word.

3.  **Searching for sounds:** ask your child to find words in a book with particular sounds, *eg* 'oo' or 'ee'.

*Playing word games with older children*

1. **How many words?** Choose a long word on a cereal packet or in a magazine. Help your child to make as many different words as possible out of it. What do they need to use to help them? A dictionary, thesaurus, word list?
2. **Making a story.** Ask your child to cut six pictures from a magazine or find six picture postcards. They put the pictures in an order of their choosing and then have to write a story to fit the pictures.

## Teaching the alphabet

It is important that your child recognises letters but be careful how you teach them. Do not use the names of letters such as 'aiy' for 'a' or 'see' for 'c'. Instead teach the sounds – the phonics. So 'a' will be 'ah' as in cat and 'c' will be 'cuh'. This will make it easier when your child starts to join sounds together. The names of the letters will be learnt later.

## Using upper or lower case

Start teaching letters and sounds using the lower case. This helps children when they start to look at combinations of sounds. Older children who have already got a good recognition of lower case letters can be introduced to upper case (capital) letters gradually.

*Making an alphabet game*

Make a set of cards with both upper and lower case letters of the alphabet on them. Hide one half and ask your child to draw the letter in the other case.

## QUESTIONS AND ANSWERS

*My child uses either hand for holding a pencil. Should I make him use one or the other?*

Do not worry. Many children can use either hand quite happily. Eventually they will show a preference for one or the other – it doesn't matter which. Concentrate on helping your child to write clearly and to hold the pencil correctly, whichever hand he is using.

*How can I encourage my child to speak clearly?*

Tape recorders can be very useful for this. Your child will enjoy hearing his or her voice on tape. Ask them to record a story or poem. Explain that they must speak clearly because a tape recorder makes voices sound slightly different. Ask them to record a message on tape to send to a relative.

*The school has given all parents a copy of the alphabet they use. What do I do with it?*
Use it as the basis for writing words or sentences for your child to copy or trace. This will reinforce your child's recognition of the letters and will not lead to confusion between writing at home and school. Write labels to put on household objects. Do not use the upper case letters until your child is taught them at school. Never write words all in upper case letters.

## PRACTISING CREATIVE WRITING AND RECORDING

A lot of work that your child does at school, especially as they get older, will involve the ability either to record or to writer **creatively**. Creative writing can be writing poems, stories, spells, plays, *etc*. Reporting might, for example, involve recording how an experiment was conducted and what the result was, explaining how something was created, describing an object or an event. Although these seem like separate kinds of writing they have similarities. Both must be logical and clear and have a beginning and an end. The National Curriculum ensures that your child will learn how to:

- develop ideas
- communicate meaning
- use a wide vocabulary
- use different styles of writing
- organise sentences grammatically
- present correctly spelt and legible work
- use a variety of writing forms for different purposes.

Here are some ways to help your child:

- use pictures to start stories and poems
- ask your child to tell you a story and then write it
- help your child start a big scrapbook diary
- do something together and then help your child to record the process.

*Using pictures*
Pictures are a good starting point for any kind of creative writing. Use pictures that are colourful and full of detail. Don't despise the standard story opening of 'Once upon a time...'. It can be a good way to encourage your child to start a story. With poems help your child to write (or for younger children you write what they say) short statements about the picture. These can then be arranged into a poem. Explain that not all poems rhyme but that they do have a rhythm. Say the poem out loud together.

*Telling a story then writing*
If your child needs help constructing a story then ask them to tell it to you before they write it (or with younger children you can write it down as they say it). By asking them to tell you first you can help them structure it logically by asking questions such as 'And then what happened?' 'Did he like that?' 'Then where did they go?' Read the story together when it is finished.

*Making a scrapbook diary*
A diary need not be a small book with nothing but lots of writing. It can be fun and a good way of helping your child get used to recording. It need not be filled in every day, only when your child has done something special that they want to record. That way it will stay fun rather than a chore.

- Buy a large scrapbook or make one with large pieces of blank paper. Help your child decorate the cover. When they want to record something they can write it on a piece of paper and stick it in together with pictures, drawings, tickets, photos *etc*.

*Recording something you did together*
Perhaps you have been doing some cooking together, or completed a jigsaw puzzle, or planted some seeds. Whatever it was it will make an ideal subject for recording. You can sit together while you ask questions so that your child tells you what you did in the correct order. Each time you have decided what the next step was your child can write it down. With younger children you write down what your child says and then read it together.

*Using a computer*
If you have a computer let your child type out his or her writing on it. Help your child correct the spelling and then print it out. Work looks

impressive on screen and when printed. It encourages children to see their work well presented particularly if their handwriting is still poor.

## IMPROVING HANDWRITING AND SPELLING

Some schools have returned to formal lessons in spelling and handwriting. Others prefer to teach children as part of general lessons. However it is done, it is recognised that good handwriting and spelling are part of what a child needs to learn. The government has recognised this by indicating that marks should be taken off for bad spelling in GCSE exams.

Clear handwriting enables others to understand what your child is saying. Spelling helps understanding too – a wrongly spelt word can change the meaning of a sentence entirely. For example, 'The child whined' or 'The child wined'.

Some teachers prefer not to correct spelling as it occurs in children's written work because they don't want to discourage creativity. However, more and more it is being accepted that learning spelling is a valid way of proceeding.

### Improving handwriting

Before your child can write clearly he or she must be able to hold their pencil or pen correctly. It does not matter whether they prefer to use their right or left hand. Do not try to force use of the right hand if your child is naturally left handed. What matters is that the pencil is held between the thumb and first finger and resting on the second finger. Discourage your child from resting the pencil at the base of the thumb and first finger with other fingers curled over the pencil. That way (which many older children seem to have got in the habit of using) is unwieldy and makes good handwriting very difficult because there is less control over the pencil. Encourage the correct hold from the start.

Good ways to improve handwriting include:

● copying

● tracing

● drawing shape patterns.

*Copying*
Find some examples of good handwriting (there are many handwriting

books for primary children available) and allow your child to copy the letters.

*Tracing*
Draw large letters on separate sheets of paper or card. Younger children can trace these with their fingers or through tracing paper with crayons. For older children write the letters near normal size and allow them to trace them with a pencil or felt-tipped pen.

*Drawing shape patterns*
Many handwriting books have writing patterns to copy. These are related to the shapes of letters. I expect you remember some from your own childhood. You can make your own by taking a letter such as 'w' and drawing lots of it joined together for a whole row (WWWWWWWW) then drawing the same pattern upside down. Two letters joined alternately could make a different pattern *eg* 'lele'.

## Handwriting styles
Before you help your child with handwriting at home make sure that you understand which kind of handwriting the school prefers to teach. There are different ways of writing many letters and if you teach your child the wrong way he or she will become confused.

Ask your child's teacher for a copy of the handwriting alphabet the school uses. Don't try to teach joined writing until the school starts to teach the class as a whole otherwise you might get your child into bad habits. You should be reinforcing your child's efforts at learning the writing the school teaches. Any handwriting taught by the school will be clear and acceptable.

## REINFORCING UNDERSTANDING

Just teaching your child something once will not be enough. Children learn through practice and repetition. They need constant reinforcement of what they are learning so that it becomes a habit and part of what they do naturally.

But do not make reinforcement boring. Doing the same thing in the same way day after day will only put your child off. Try to introduce different ways of doing things so that your child is practising the same thing but in a different context. For example, you could ask your child to help you read a poster, write down a recipe, copy a poem for an aunty, write a letter to a pen friend or write a story to read to a younger sibling.

wwwwwwwwwwwwwwwwwwwwwwwwwwwwwwwww

qbqbqbqbqbqbqbqbqbqbqbqbqb

edbeedbeedbeedbeedbeedbeedb

nnnnnnnnnnnnnnnnnnnnnnnnnnnnnnnn

UUUUUUUUUUUUUUUUUUUUUUUUUUU

nununununununununununununun

ssssssssssssssssssssssssssssssssss

xxxxxxxxxxxxxxxxxxxxxxxxxxxxxx

ofofofofofofofofofofofofofoofo

oxoxoxooxoxoxoxoxoxoxoxoxoxo

Fig. 2. Handwriting patterns

46

Think of ways of introducing what the child has learned into everyday situations. The more relevant the skills seem to the child the more they will want to learn and practise them.

## CASE STUDIES

### Sally and Geoff write a story

Geoff can write his name and a few words such as 'a' and 'and'. He is keen to write a story so Sally helps him. She asks Geoff to tell her a story. He tells her the Three Bears starting 'Once upon a time...'. As he tells it Sally asks questions then writes down the sentence Geoff says. She writes the letters in pencil the way the school has shown her and leaves lots of space between the lines. When they have finished Geoff writes over the words with a black pen. Some of the words he copies underneath. When he has finished he writes his name. He is so pleased that he draws a picture and insists on reading the story to Sally every night for a week!

### Becky writes to grandma

Becky likes writing but being shy doesn't like showing the teacher her work because her handwriting is 'wobbly' (it looks fine to everyone else). Mary asks Becky to write to Grandma to tell her about their new pet rabbit. Becky doesn't mind writing to Grandma because Grandma lives a long way away. Grandma (suitably primed) writes back to Becky (in very clear writing) and tells her how interesting her letter was and how neat the handwriting is. Becky is thrilled to get a letter of her own and Mary helps her read it. To encourage her Mary asks her to copy the letter onto the school computer.

### Harry helps both sons with reading

Harry thinks that Eddy needs to be stretched more with his reading while Mark needs lots of practice to keep up with his year. The trouble is that it is difficult to help both of them without one becoming bored or jealous. Harry reads stories to them that they can both enjoy. Once a day he hears them both read separately.

Eddy likes reading and writing and is only too keen to practise but Mark is not bothered. Harry takes him aside one day and asks him if he would like to go and see a football match. Mark is thrilled but Harry says he must write to ask for tickets himself. He helps Mark compose the letter and then stays with him while he writes it. He sends it with the money (and a covering letter) to the ticket office. Mark is thrilled to get the tickets in the post a few days later and both boys enjoy the match.

## SUMMARY

● Encourage speaking and listening.

● Try to hear your child read for a few minutes every day.

● Give lots of praise and encouragement.

● Help your child to write and record.

● Make handwriting practice fun.

● Reinforce understanding through repetition.

# 4

## Improving Mathematical Skills

Maths for primary aged children is largely based on real life. It:

- is practical

- is relevant to real life

- is about solving problems

- involves discussion.

Different children develop at different stages but by the ages of 7 and 11 they should be using certain maths skills. By about 7 years children should understand the language of numbers, properties of shapes and comparatives, *eg* 'bigger than', 'next to', 'before'. They should be able to relate numbers and maths symbols, *eg* +, −, ÷, × to various situations and, to recognise simple patterns and make predictions about them.

By 11 years children should also understand and use the language of:

- movements of shapes

- simple probability

- measures and relationships including 'multiple of' (a number is a multiple of another if the second number divides into the first with no remainder, *eg* six is a multiple of three), 'factor of' (one of two or more numbers which when multiplied together make the answer), 'symmetrical to' *eg* exactly the same on both sides of a straight line.

They should also be able to use diagrams, graphs and simple algebraic symbols.

Children of all ages should be developing mathematical reasoning by asking questions and investigating at appropriate levels. Remember these guidelines are for the average child. Bear them in mind as you read this chapter and when choosing activities and language to use with your child.

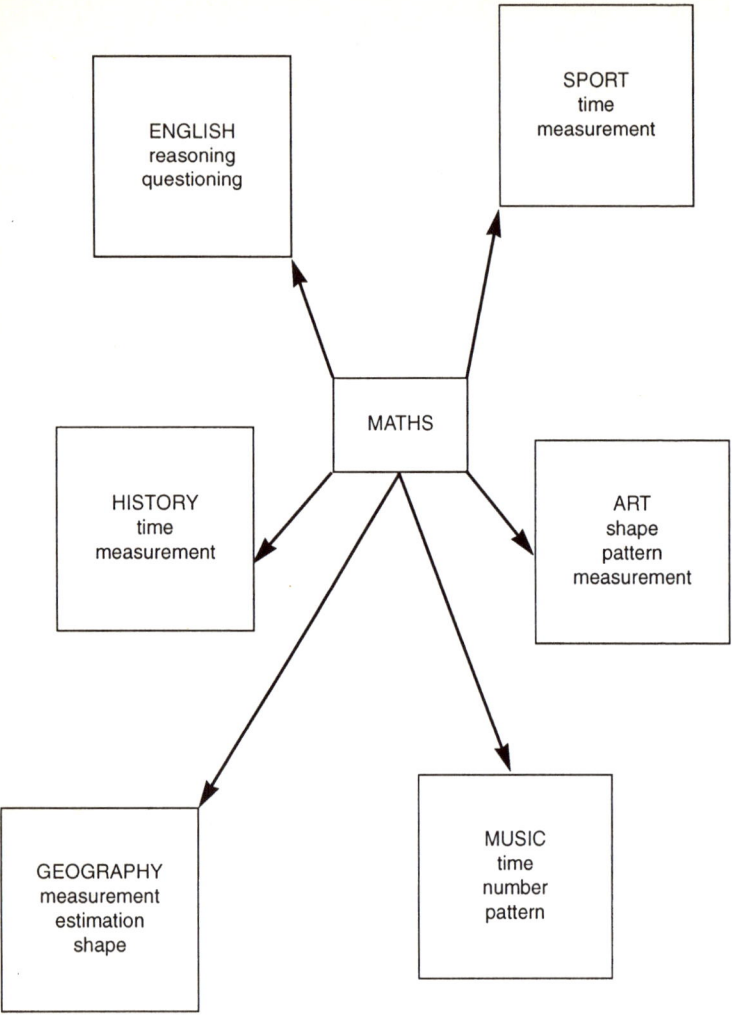

Fig. 3. Using maths in other subjects.

## USING MATHS IN EVERYDAY LIFE

Maths is more than just numbers. It involves position and pattern, the relationship of one thing or number to another. It is part of so many everyday activities that you and your children understand a lot about it already. For example, just by walking to the shops together you are taking part in a simple measurement exercise. Is it a long way? A short way? Longer than the walk to school?

## Learning maths together

Children need to learn the basics of maths, that is the 'building blocks', as soon as possible and to continue to use them and enlarge on them throughout life. You can help them by:

- developing your child's maths skills

- encouraging mathematical talk

- encouraging mathematical thinking

- helping develop your child's maths thinking

- making maths a part of your lives

- encouraging questions to make them mathematically aware

- supporting a positive attitude.

## Finding maths in the home

You can find ways of using and finding out about maths everywhere. First look around your home. For example:

- kitchen – *eg* weighing, cost of ingredients, temperatures

- bathroom *eg* weight (what sinks and what doesn't)

- bedroom – *eg* measurement (how wide is the cupboard, why does one toy racing car go faster than another?)

- dining room – shape, geometry (shape of table, door, window, place mats, how rectangular place mats fit together on the table).

Don't forget that lots of games can help your child learn maths while he or she plays. Some games have versions for younger and older children. These are some games that are fun and relevant to maths:

- ludo

- dominoes

- draughts

- Monopoly

- snakes and ladders

- jigsaw puzzles and shape games (*eg* Tangram)

● card games.

Here are examples of activities at home with a mathematical content.

*Chinese Egg and Tangram*
Younger children can try the Egg and older ones the Tangram. Mark the shapes of the Egg and Tangram on paper and cut the shapes out carefully. See how many pictures you can make from both. How many different bird shapes can you make from the egg? How many different pictures can you make from the Tangram? Can you put the Egg and Tangram back together?

*Calendar questions*
Use a large calendar as the basis for questions. Vary the questions according to the age of the child. How many weeks is it till your birthday? Which day of the week is it? What will be the date next Thursday? How many Mondays are there in September? How long is the summer holiday?

*Buttons*
Younger children can sort the buttons into different sets, *eg* coloured, plain, large, small, number of holes *etc*. Now sort the sets in different ways, *eg* by how they are used. Are any buttons in both sets? Older children can count the buttons and sort them into piles of *eg* four (or five or six *etc*). How many piles are there? How many buttons are left over?

## Making maths outdoors

You can find maths outdoors too. When you go out and about with your child be alert for opportunities to use maths. For example:

● shopping – *eg* calculating cost, amount, weight

● in the park – *eg* measurement, speed (running, walking, on bike)

● at the swimming pool – *eg* speed, length, time.

Here are some examples of the way you can introduce maths to your child when you are out together.

*Spotting pub signs*
Each limb on a pub sign counts as one point. So The Fox and Goose = six and The Green Man four. You and your child can play. The first person to reach 50 points wins.

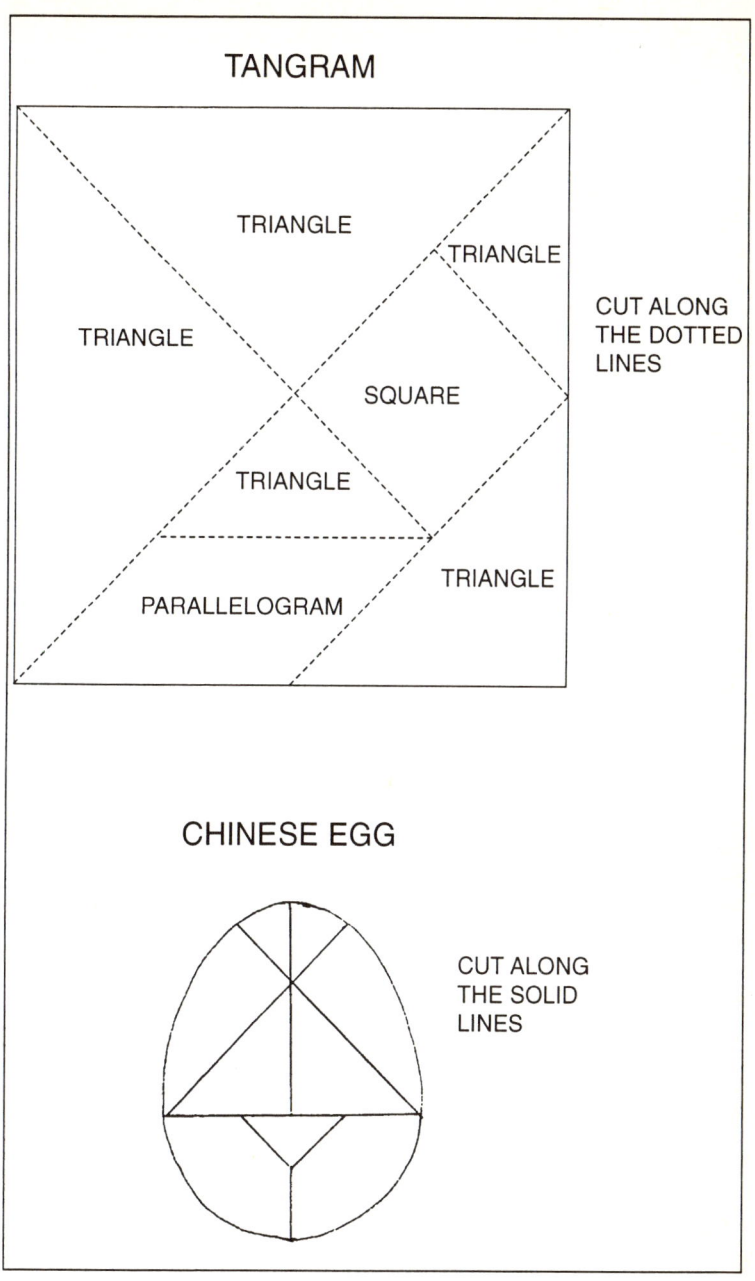

## TANGRAM

TRIANGLE

TRIANGLE

TRIANGLE

SQUARE

TRIANGLE

TRIANGLE

PARALLELOGRAM

CUT ALONG
THE DOTTED
LINES

## CHINESE EGG

CUT ALONG
THE SOLID
LINES

Figure 4. Tangram and Chinese Egg puzzles.

*In the park*
While your child is playing ask questions like these: How far can you run/cycle in one minute? Two minutes? How many slides can you do in two minutes? Can you do twice as many in four minutes? How long does it take to go round on the roundabout six times?

*Making house number sums*
Make sure your child understands that there are odd numbers on one side of the road and even on the other. Younger children can say the numbers and when they can't see the next one, tell you what it will be. With older children tell them that the numbers on two neighbouring houses total, *eg* ten. What are the numbers on the doors? If the total is eight what are the two numbers? How can you work this out quickly?

## PRACTISING BASIC MATHS SKILLS
Help your child improve his or her basic maths skills. By:

- using maths in practical tasks
- practising problem solving
- learning mathematical language
- developing mathematical reasoning.

### Using maths in practical tasks
Introduce maths into your everyday activities as suggested elsewhere in this chapter. Give your child opportunities to do practical tasks, *eg* building, weighing, recording, sorting, *etc*. This makes maths meaningful and fun.

### Practising problem solving
There are lots of ways of doing things and of solving problems that occur in everyday life. Is there another way to measure the garden? Which is the easiest way to work out the price of seven cans of soup? Encourage your children to solve problems. Let them use ways they are happy with but encourage them to look for other solutions too. This way you will be helping them develop the problem solving skills that are such an important part of maths.

Don't solve the problems for your child. Help them get started and then let them try the activity for themselves. Ask questions to help them, *eg*:

● Why do you think that piece won't fit? What else can you try? Why?

● What happens when you add those five sets of buttons together? Is there another way of doing it?

## Learning mathematical language

You use mathematical language every day with your children without being aware of it. Here are some examples:

● high, higher, highest

● low, lower, lowest

● next to, beside, between

● under, below, above, over

● long, longer, longest

● short, shorter, shortest

● heavy, heavier, heaviest

● light, lighter, lightest.

Don't be afraid to use proper names for Mathematical terms when appropriate:

● square, rectangle, octagon, pentagon, hexagon, oval, triangle

● cube, pyramid, sphere

● multiply, divide, add, subtract

● grams, kilograms

● centimetres, metres

● litres.

By using mathematical language with your child you make it a natural part of their life and they begin to learn and use it themselves.

## Developing mathematical reasoning

Maths is about working things out and making deductions. You can help your child do this by asking them to explain how and why they are doing something. You can also get them to show you how they work something out by recording the steps they took on paper or a calculator. The practice with estimating and calculating suggested elsewhere in this chapter will also help them.

## Reading helps maths

At school children practise their maths skills by using written examples and problems on cards, paper, in books or on a computer. So reading skills are important in maths. Speaking skills are important too because children need to be able to describe problems and explain how they solve them. If you help your child with language skills, as described in Chapter 3, you will be supporting your child's mathematical skills too.

## Using the four signs

The basic skills useful for maths are much wider than learning to use add, subtract, multiply and divide. But many parents are concerned about children using these signs. Before you help your child do sums using the signs please ask your child's teacher how the school does the calculations. There can be variations in the way a sum is set out or a multiplication sum is worked out, for example.

*Encouraging understanding*

Help your child to understand the maths in any activity. It does not have to be complicated. You simply talk to them about what they are doing and ask questions about it. Which swing is going higher? Do six small apples weigh more than three large ones? What happens when you try to fit octagonal place mats together to cover the table? Why?

## QUESTIONS AND ANSWERS

*I always hated maths. How can I help my own child?*

Maths today is fun because it relates to everyday things and you will find that you enjoy helping your own child through play. Play games and read books with a maths content. Involve your child in everyday activities and use maths language to talk about what you are doing. Solve practical problems together. You will learn some maths too and it will enhance your relationship with your child.

*Learning tables was important when I was at school. Should I get my children to learn their tables by rote?*

Learning tables is important today too, but not all schools teach children their tables by rote. If you want to help your children learn their tables make it fun. Buy a tape with the tables set to music so that they can sing along with it. Or buy them a book with the tables illustrated with cartoons. But more importantly, help your child understand how numbers work by using them in a practical way.

*My child's teacher doesn't want me to teach any maths at home. What can I do?*

Some teachers worry that you might try to teach your child formal maths or maths of an inappropriate standard. But you can help your child with maths without making them sit down and do sums. Use mathematical language in ordinary situations and talk through problems together. Use books and games with a maths content to introduce maths ideas without formally 'teaching' them. Your child will improve maths skills and enjoy doing it without realising it.

## ESTIMATING AND CALCULATING

A lot of maths involves making a guess about what the answer to a problem might be and then working out an answer and comparing the two. Children need to do a lot of estimation in maths – making an 'educated guess'. By doing this they start to understand how to work answers out and to understand maths in a practical way. The more they estimate, the closer their guesses will be to the right answer. It will help them judge whether their calculations are likely to be right or wrong.

You can help by following these steps in problem solving:

1. Ask questions about a problem – *eg* 'How long do you think our garden is?' or 'What number do you think the answer will be?'

2. Help your child choose an appropriate means to do the job, *eg* 'How can we measure the garden? Shall we use hands or paces?' or 'How can you work that out? Is multiplying or adding best? Is there another way?'

3. Help your child solve the problem. 'Let's count the paces as we walk along the garden' or 'Show me how you will write the sum out. Do you want to check it with your calculator?'

4. Encourage your child to compare the estimate and the answer – *eg* 'We counted 27 paces. You guessed 36. Was that too many or too few paces?' or 'That's very good. You estimated 316 and the answer was 345. Can you estimate the next number?'

Here are some things your child can estimate:

- length – how far along, across, wide, deep?
- height
- weight – how much does it weigh, how heavy is it?

- shape – how many will fit it, cover it, will fit together?

- number – can you guess/estimate: seven lots of two apples, 19 lots of biscuits with 23 in each packet, the distance to school plus the distance to the shops, the number of buttons in the box?

## MANAGING A CALCULATOR

Children like using calculators. They make working out problems easy and quick. But the government has now decided that children under eight should not be encouraged to use them. This is because it is important that young children understand how maths works. Until they have the basic maths skills how can they:

1. Tell if an answer on a calculator is right?

2. Work out where they went wrong in the method of calculating?

Younger children can play with a calculator for fun. Children of junior school age can start to use calculators for working out problems. Don't let them work out all the answers on a calculator. Get them to do some calculations with pen and paper first and then use the calculator to check. Ask them to explain how they are doing it and why they know the answer is right.

### Calculator games

Children aged seven or eight or older can have fun playing games with their calculators such as those described below.

*The target game*
Choose any two numbers between one and nine. Choose a target number between ten and 20. You can use add and subtract and the equals sign. You can use your two numbers as many times as you like. Try to make a sum that reaches the target number, or as close as possible. So if your numbers were eight and three and your target number was 15 you could make sums like eight add eight add eight subtract three subtract three subtract three equals 15, or three add three add three add three add three equals 15. How few key strokes can you use? Try sums using equals, subtract and multiply or all four function keys.

*Two keys only*
Using numbers five and seven only and all the function keys – plus,

subtract, multiply, divide – try to make all the numbers from one to 20 *eg* To make 12 the sum would be five add seven equals 12.

*Pocket money game*
Imagine your pocket money is just one penny every week but that it doubles every week. How much is it in week one, two, three, four *etc*. When does the calculation get hard enough to use a calculator? When does the amount of money reach more than £20? £50? £100?

## CHOOSING AND USING MATHS BOOKS

You do not need special books to help your child with maths. So do not rush out and buy lots of traditional 'sums' books immediately. But there are several kinds of book that are useful.

### Choosing maths books
The most useful books will not be full of sums but will give you ideas about the kind of maths activities you can do with your child. Other books which can help are story books with a mathematical idea behind them (see Further Reading).

Here are some other ideas for books that will support your child's maths – often without them realising. For younger children:

● nursery rhymes

● simple counting books

● 'mirror' books (symmetry).

For older children:

● maths dictionary

● maths puzzle books

● brain teasers

● maths based quiz books

● books of mazes

● books about kites (shape).

Before you buy a maths book for your child to use at home you should make sure that it is appropriate for your child's age. Try the following suggestions to get advice.

*Asking the teacher*
Ask your child's teacher what kind of books would be useful for your child. If possible have a look at the ones in your child's classroom and school library.

*Asking a librarian*
The librarian in the children's section of your local library will be able to answer your questions about choosing relevant books. Don't be afraid of sounding silly. Librarians are there to help and enjoy advising parents about relevant books. Take your child along too.

*Asking your friends*
You may have friends with children about your children's age. If so, ask them what kinds of books their children enjoy, especially with a maths content. Borrow them, swop for them or buy them or use your local library to order them.

*Using this book*
In the Further Reading section at the back of this book I have listed some books suitable for the two age groups.

## Using maths books

Story books, counting books, puzzle books can be read passively or actively. Story books can be used to prompt questions and explanations. Puzzle books, quiz books, books on mazes *etc* all require a response. By reading them with your child you can encourage them to involve themselves with maths actively.

You should:

● read with them

● talk about it

● ask questions

● ask your child to explain the content.

## Buying 'sums' books

You don't have to use traditional 'sums' maths books. If you want your child to record calculations then any paper will do. Often large pieces are needed for such things as diagrams, charts, pictures *etc*.

If you think your child would enjoy using formal maths books choose them carefully and do not use them too often. Your child's teacher will be giving them all the formal maths they need and will set any maths homework necessary. Get advice first.

1. Ask the advice of your child's teacher. The school might prefer parents not to use the same books as it does or would prefer you to use supplementary ones or none.

2. Buy maths books published by a publisher with a good reputation for educational books. Ask the teacher or a librarian.

3. Take into account the age of your child. The book will tell you what age range it is suitable for or will tell you the key stages of the curriculum it is suitable for. In that case remember that:

   ● Key Stage 1 = 5–7 years (year groups 1 and 2)

   ● Key Stage 2 = 7–11 years (year groups 3–6).

Older children can do maths puzzles with your help or play quiz games. Make using the books fun. Reading and language skills develop too. Many of the books you choose should encourage children to do things for themselves.

## CASE STUDIES

### Sally and Geoff play games
Geoff's teacher has told Sally that the best way she can support Geoff's maths at home is to use language and play to help him become aware of position and pattern in everyday life. 'Board games are helpful, and fun too' she adds. Sally already takes Geoff to the park and the swimming pool. She now tries to introduce more mathematical language while he plays. She borrows story books with maths themes from the local library and introduces them for bedtime stories. When they are at home she and Geoff play games with a maths content such as simple ludo or picture dominoes. Her friend Annie has twin girls of Geoff's age and lends Sally a construction toy for a few weeks. Geoff thinks all this is great fun but he is quickly improving his grasp of mathematical language and is beginning to try to solve problems by explaining them to Sally.

### Robert and Mary buy a computer
Robert and Mary save up for a second hand computer and some maths computer games recommended by Becky's teacher. The games have lots

of cartoon characters and require responses from Becky to learn mathematical concepts and solve problems on the screen. Becky is allowed to play with the computer for an hour each evening as long as she chooses at least one maths game. Robert and Mary help Becky use the computer the first few times and introduce her to the games. Becky quickly doesn't need their help and loves 'playing' the maths games. Not only does her maths improve but her confidence grows. At the next parents' evening her teacher tells Robert and Mary that Becky now talks more in class and takes her share of using the computer. She even explains to other children how to use it.

## Harry makes a mistake

Harry is so keen to give Eddy harder maths that he buys a lot of 'sums' books and makes Eddy sit down and spend an hour a night working on them. Meanwhile he encourages Mark to play football with his friends to try and get into the school team. But Eddy quickly gets bored with being forced to do sums every night and Mark resents the attention Eddy is getting with his school work. Eddy starts to  lose interest in maths at school and Mark gives up trying altogether. Harry eventually realises his mistake and contacts Eddy and Mark's teachers. Eddy's teacher recommends some games and story books that will help Eddy enjoy maths. Mark's teacher suggests that Harry takes both boys to the swimming pool and to some of Mark's football games. He can introduce mathematical language to both boys – faster, length, speed, number in teams *etc*. Mark will feel wanted and both boys will learn. Harry spends some extra time with Mark on his own to reassure Mark that he is just as important. Both boys feel less pressured and begin to enjoy learning again.

## SUMMARY

- Make maths part of your everyday life.

- Learning maths together is fun.

- Use maths language in everyday situations in the home and outdoors.

- Use books and games with a maths content.

- Help your child improve language skills; they are important for maths.

- Help your child practise the basics maths skills – using maths language, developing maths reasoning, solving problems.

- Help your child practise estimating and calculating.

- Be positive about maths and make it fun.

# 5

## Supporting Science Skills

Science for primary school children is related to the world they can see around them. It is an exciting part of their lives. Think about the natural world, how cars work, space programs, the wonders of the stars – to name but a few things.

Your child would lose out on much that makes life fascinating if he or she failed to learn about scientific things. And as you help your child with this exciting subject together you too will learn more about how our world works.

### Learning science in primary school
Primary school science will teach your child to:

- use scientific vocabulary

- present scientific information

- understand scientific ideas

- evaluate evidence

- follow basic safety rules.

During the primary school years he or she will learn about:

- how to experiment and investigate

- living things and processes – plants, animals, humans

- materials and properties

- physical processes – electricity, forces and motion, light and sound, the earth and beyond.

Science in primary school tends to be taught in an integrated way. That means that instead of separate biology, physics and chemistry lessons, science subjects are taught together as part of project work. So your child might do a physics experiment to see whether wood or metal floats and then use maths to work out how heavy each piece is by weighing it. Or perhaps your child will combine geography in drawing a simple map of the school playing field and then looking at the flowers around the edge and studying how they are made.

As children progress through the primary school then experiments become more separated out.

## FINDING SCIENCE EVERYWHERE

Helping your child with science means helping him or her become more observant about the world around us. You may already have encountered questions from your child such as 'Why is the sky blue?' 'How do whales breathe?' 'Why does wood float?' 'Where does gas come from?' 'How do planes stay up in the air?'. These are all science questions.

### Looking for science

Science is all about you. Everything that you can see, hear, touch, smell or taste (and some that you can't) is science. When you are taking your child for a walk the trees and flowers you see, the tarmac on the road, the birds and cars you hear are all part of the scientific world. Even the ice creams you buy have been perfected by chemistry experiments!

So part of the way you can support your child's science education is by letting him or her know that virtually everything has some scientific basis and that it is therefore endlessly fascinating.

## OBSERVING AND RECORDING

Part of any science based work is learning to look carefully, to observe what something is like or what happens and then to record those observations. This is the basis of all experiments or science studies. Without careful observation and accurate recording it is impossible to draw conclusions about what happened, that is, to get a 'result'

The stages in science studies are:

1. Define what you are trying to do (*ie* describe what you are looking for).

2. Prepare the experiment or work out what you are going to be observing.

3. Observe carefully.

4. Record what you saw, what happened.

5. Come to a conclusion about the result.

All this might sound daunting but really it is very straightforward. It involves helping your child to look and record.

## DOING EXPERIMENTS

As mentioned above experiments are usually done in a logical sequence. The sequence is based on asking questions about each stage of the process. You and your child don't have to ask difficult questions.

Examples of experiments might be:

● weighing

● measuring

● water experiments.

*Weighing*
Discovering whether things weigh the same or differently is the basis of many primary experiments. You can use practically anything for this. You can also introduce simple weighing with weights when you ask your child to help you do some cooking. With younger children you would show them the weight to put on and then help them put the ingredient into the opposite pan until the weights balanced. With older children you could ask them to find the correct weights and weigh out the ingredients or provide simple written instructions.

*Measuring*
This is a part of most experiments. Weighing too is a form of measurement. Your child needs to learn the most appropriate unit of measurement for the task. So, for example, a distance can't be measured in grams.

*Water experiments*
Many measuring and weighing experiments can be done with water. It also gives the opportunity of doing floating/sinking experiments – always great fun for both children and parents! And messy – so make sure the floor is adequately covered and that you and the child wear big aprons.

## Doing an experiment
Now that you and your child have chosen an activity with an experimental aspect you need to know how to do it. Experiments can be very simple but they all teach children something about the way the world works.

*Defining the problem*
This usually means asking a question such as 'Does wood float?', 'Is flour heavier or lighter than marbles?', 'Which rolls down a hill quicker – a sphere or a cylinder?' and so on.

By asking a question your child is halfway to working out how to find the answer.

*Preparing the experiment*
Again your child can do this (with your help) by asking questions. For example, 'What rolls downhill faster – a sphere (or a ball) or a cylinder?' You can ask your child what are they going to roll down? We haven't got a hill. Together you could decide to build a wooden ramp and then to use a small ball and a rolling pin to roll down it.

*Observing carefully*
The next part of an experiment is important. You have to do the experiment and watch carefully what happens. In the example above your child would hold the ball and the rolling pin at the top of the ramp and let them go together. Then you would see what happened. Did the ball or the rolling pin reach the bottom first? You might try it ten times to see whether it ever changed.

*Recording the result*
Your child needs to get into the habit of recording the result of an experiment. It can be done very easily. In the rolling example above you could ask your child to draw a ball and a rolling pin at the top of a sheet of paper. Every time the ball reached the bottom of the ramp first they could put a tick under the ball picture; likewise for the rolling pin.

*Reaching a conclusion*
This means looking at the results of the experiment and deciding what they mean. So, for example, if there were more ticks or only ticks under the ball picture our child could decide that balls (spheres) roll down slopes faster than rolling pins (cylinders). Older children could write this on the paper; younger children could tell you. They could also try to answer 'why?' This is more difficult but is a good way for them to get

used to trying to describe something in detail. For example, they might reply that (if true) a ball rolls faster because it is fatter and not much of it touches the slope.

## DISCOVERING THE LIVING WORLD

Plants, trees, animals, birds, fish, people, are all part of the living world and come under the heading 'science'. Most children have a genuine fascination with living things. Together you can discover the interesting things about them.

In school your child might do some or all of the following, among many other things:

- look after a class pet

- grow plants

- contribute to a nature table

- visit a park/zoo/nature reserve.

You and your child can discover the living world around you together. Don't just show your child things, talk about them. You can follow up any particular interests in books and on videos.

Classes in primary schools often have a nature table where items from the natural world are displayed. The children are asked to contribute to the table which constantly changes according to what is brought in and the season. You can help your child look out for items to take into class for the table as you go on walks together.

### Finding the natural world

Start with your own back garden or yard. Don't assume because you are not a good gardener that there is nothing of interest in it. Even a weed is part of the natural world and can be used to learn about growth, decay, and how a plant is made up. If you haven't got a garden a pot plant or a window box will do!

Here are some other suggestions for places you can find the natural world with your child:

- park

- zoo

- wildlife park

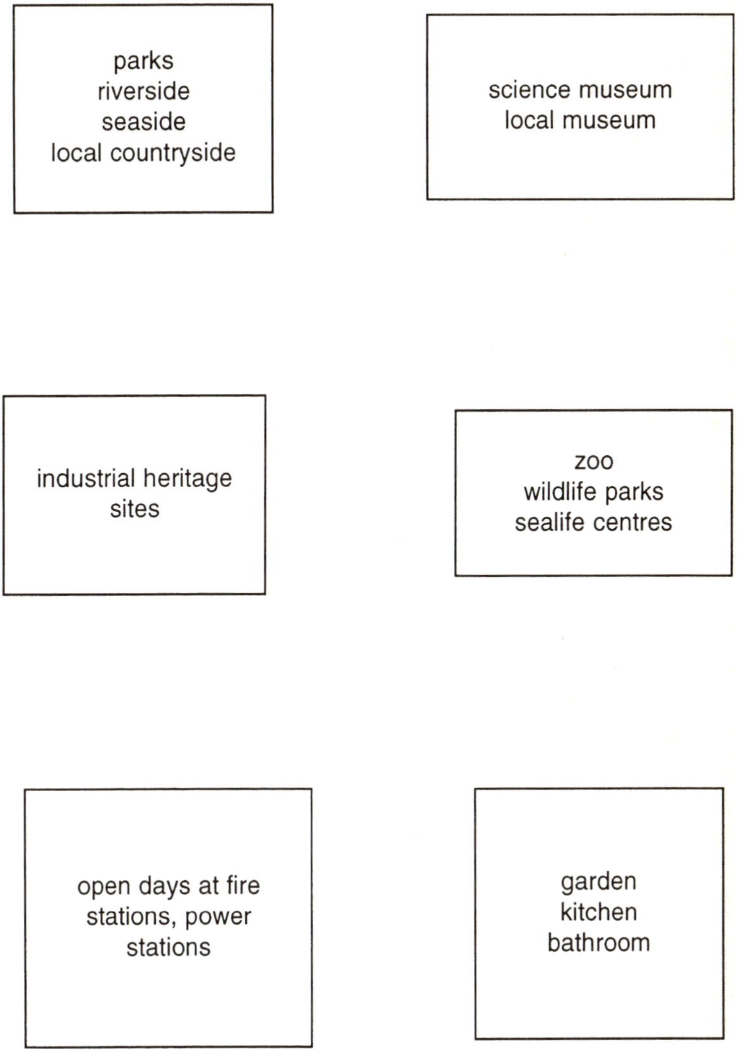

parks
riverside
seaside
local countryside

science museum
local museum

industrial heritage
sites

zoo
wildlife parks
sealife centres

open days at fire
stations, power
stations

garden
kitchen
bathroom

Fig. 5. Finding science.

- botanical garden

- commons

- seaside

- sealife centre

- riverside.

## BRINGING SCIENCE HOME

At school your child will be introduced to as much of the living world as possible. You can help by following up some of the work done in school and your child's interests. For example, one primary teacher told the class about birds. The children were asked to draw birds they had seen. One child was so interested that he spent every evening and weekend watching the birds in his garden and drawing them. His mother asked the teacher to recommend a simple book about birds so that she could foster his interest. She helped him join a bird watching club too so that he could learn more about them. Both she and her son enjoyed trips together to many different places to see birds.

*Living creatures*
Most primary classes have a pet or share a pet with other classes. It teaches children about how animals or birds live and what they need to stay alive and happy. It also teaches the related skills of caring and consideration and how living things depend on one another. It also teaches them the reality of life – illness, death, procreation *etc.*

At the end of each term it is common for the teacher to ask if anyone can look after the class pet for the holiday. If possible allow your child to do so at least once. It is quite a responsibility to be in sole charge of an animal, bird or fish without other children or the teacher to help. You can help your child by making sure that the creature is fed, watered, cleaned and played with safely during the holiday period.

*Having your own pet*
You might not have room for a pet or be in accommodation where pets are not allowed. If so, see whether you can find a friend or neighbour with a pet who would be willing to allow your child to 'help' with them. Perhaps you could offer to take a neighbour's dog for regular walks which your child could go on too, or maybe a friend has a bird that needs cleaning out and playing with once a week.

If you can have a pet, and can afford one, it does not have to be large. Dogs and cats are popular but so are guinea pigs, rabbits, gerbils, hamsters, white rats, mice *etc*. Don't try to keep wild animals like hedgehogs in your home because it is illegal and they will pine.

Consider other types of pet too – a budgie, a tortoise, goldfish, or even stick insects. These are less difficult to deal with than the usual pets although they each have their problems. You need to be able to afford to feed your pet. If you can't afford vets' fees the nearest Blue Cross or PDSA will treat your animal for free or for a small fee. The local dog or cat home might give you an animal if they think it will go to a loving home, or a friend might be able to give you an unwanted pet. Before you get any pet for your child remember:

1. Make sure you can afford to feed it and take it to the vet.

2. Get a type of pet your child really likes.

3. Make sure that you are prepared to supervise the pet's cleaning and feeding.

4. Don't buy a pet that is clearly unsuitable for your home, *eg* an Alsatian in a small tower block flat.

5. Be sure that you will be prepared to look after the pet for as long as it lives.

6. Be sure that you and your child are willing to give the pet the activities it needs, *eg* a daily walk for a dog.

*Growing plants*
Children of all ages are usually fascinated by growing things. At school they will grow bulbs and seeds and perhaps help plant trees in a school garden.

You can do the same at home. Here are some suggestions:

● Grow a bean in blotting paper. Put blotting paper round the inside of a jam jar and push a bean between the paper and the glass. Keep the paper damp and watch the root and shoot grow.

● Put carrot tops in a saucer of water and watch the tops sprout fronds.

● Plant some indoor bulbs or grow a spider plant.

● Sow some seeds in a window box or the garden. Keep the spot weeded!

- Plant an acorn, sycamore seed or conker in a large flowerpot outdoors and watch a tree grow.

## QUESTIONS AND ANSWERS

*Should I do formal science experiments with my child?*
You do not need to do formal experiments. Encourage your child to ask questions about the world round about. For example, why does cardboard bend? Why do holly trees stay green in winter? Help him or her find sources of information that will provide answers.

*My child doesn't seem interested in the natural world. How can I encourage an interest?*
Don't worry. Your child will absorb a lot of information about the world around just by living. Use television and video programmes as a fun way to provide information.

*Is science dangerous?*
An important part of science education in primary school is ensuring that children learn how to handle materials and tools safely. The teacher will ensure that all children follow the safety rules and wear any protective clothing such as goggles that might be necessary.

## CASE STUDIES

### Geoff wants a hamster
Geoff comes home from school desperately wanting a hamster. 'I love the school hamster, Mummy. Can I have one at home? I can keep it in my room.' Sally thinks they could manage a hamster but wants to make sure that Geoff is really keen on one. She arranges with the teacher to take the class pet home for the Easter holiday. Geoff is thrilled – for the first week. He isn't keen on cleaning the cage out though, and forgets to feed the hamster unless reminded. After playing with it every day for a week he then forgets about it altogether. Sally decides that Geoff isn't ready for a hamster. She offers a goldfish instead – 'until you're a bit bigger'. Geoff is happy with the goldfish because he can say he has a pet; Sally is happy to have an easily manageable pet.

## Becky does the cooking

Becky often 'helps' Robert and Mary with cooking at weekends. One Saturday they decide to make a cake for Becky's Grandma. 'How do you know how much flour to use?' Becky asks. Mary shows her the recipe and explains how to use it. 'What makes cakes rise?' asks Becky. 'Air' replies Mary. 'But how does it do it?' Mary and Robert look at each other. Robert decides to look for a science book in the library that can answer Becky's questions – he can't!

## Mark and Eddy sneak in a mouse

Mark and Eddy go to stay with a friend overnight. The next day they spend a lot of time in their room. Harry goes up to see why they are so quiet and finds them playing with a white mouse. 'Where did that come from?' he asks. It turns out that the friend's pet mouse had been breeding and he wanted to get rid of one of the mice. Mark smuggled it home in his coat pocket. 'Please can we keep it?' the boys cry. Harry gives in but says they must get a proper cage and that the boys must clean and feed it themselves – he makes sure they do.

## SUMMARY

- Look for science everywhere.

- Make learning about the world around us fun.

- Take your child on visits to zoos, nature reserves and other places of interest.

- If you buy your child a pet ensure that it will be well cared for.

- Encourage your child to grow plants.

# 6

## Discovering Geography and History

Geography, learning about the surface of the earth and its inhabitants, and history, learning about the past, are often combined. They can also encompass many other subjects. For example, history and geography can both use maths, English and art.

## LEARNING GEOGRAPHY AND HISTORY IN PRIMARY SCHOOL

Geography and history are not dry as dust subjects. An understanding of them is part of making sense of the world around us. What is dull about learning about how people lived in the past or the inhabitants of a foreign country?

At primary level teachers are provided with a number of modules with different subjects. They can pick a certain number of them to teach to their class. But because both geography and history involve so many other subjects they are taught in an integrated way.

### Learning geography

Geography in primary schools gives children the opportunity to:

- find out about physical and human features of their environment

- learn to ask geographical questions, *eg* 'How did it happen like this?'

- become aware of the wider world.

Children will develop skills relevant to geography. At the appropriate ages they will learn how to:

- use geographical terms, *eg* hill, road

- do field work, *eg* map the school playground

- use measuring equipment, *eg* a rain gauge

- use atlases, maps, plans, globes

- use secondary sources, *eg* photographs, books.

At Key Stage 1 children undertake a study of the quality of their local environment. At Key Stage 2 they study:

- rivers
- the weather
- settlements, *eg* towns, villages
- environmental change.

The studies they do will help develop geographical skills and help them learn about:

- their local environment
- unfamiliar places
- location and spatial relationships (where things are and where they are in relation to other things).

*Asking questions*
Help your child ask questions about their environment such as:

- Where is it located?
- Why has it been located here?
- What movements occur between these places?
- What are the routes linking these places, *etc*?

Again the National Curriculum provides areas of study that the teacher can choose. Often geography is combine with history in topic work.

## Learning history
History in the primary school involves:

- real people and events in the past
- sequence, time and chronology
- primary and secondary evidence.

*Real people and events in the past*
Children can learn about real people in the past. This includes how ordinary people lived as well as famous people. History shows us how people in the past and events of the past such as the Norman Conquest or the Roman invasion of Britain affected each other.

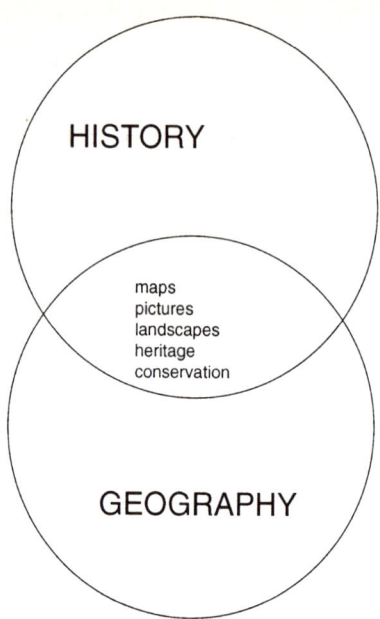

maps
pictures
landscapes
heritage
conservation

Fig. 6. History and geography combining primary school work.

*Sequence, time, chronology*
Children need to learn about the sequence of things, that is which things happened before and after other things, to develop a sense of chronology. Time is about how long events took and the time between them.

*Primary and secondary evidence*
Primary evidence is the immediate evidence of the past such as landscape, buildings, archaeological remains, reminiscences of the past (oral history), pictures, photos, films *etc*. Secondary evidence is the books about the past by historians.

All children at primary school will learn the history skills of:

- chronology

- historical knowledge and understanding

- different interpretations of history

- how to find out about the past

- how to organise their work.

Your child won't be able to learn all this at primary school but will be able to understand about many people and events in the past and will learn to handle simple primary evidence.

## Using the history syllabus
At Key Stage 1 children learn about:

- everyday lives of ordinary people in the past, including their own families

- the lives of famous people in the past

- past events, *eg* the Gunpowder Plot.

At Key Stage 2 children will learn about:

- important developments and episodes in Britain's past

- Roman to modern times in Britain and other parts of the world

- developing chronological framework

- local history.

These things will be learnt in **study units**. At present these are:

1. Romans, Anglo-Saxons or Vikings.

2. Life in Tudor times.

3. Victorian Britain or Britain since 1930.

4. Ancient Greece.

5. Local history.

6. A past non-European society.

Together you and your child can explore the past and develop the skills needed to understand it.

Younger children are taught history as part of integrated studies. Older children start to get taught history separated out occasionally into individual blocks of time. History in primary school is often studied through integrated project work where history, geography, art and other subjects all play their part.

## Helping with history
You do not have to know a lot about history to help your child. For

example, suppose the school project is family history and your child has been asked to contribute to it. You could do the following:

● help your child find photos of the family, especially older members

● take your child to visit older relatives and help them make a tape recording of their recollections

● find things to take in that belonged to your family in the past, *eg* something belonging to your child's grandfather

● take your child to visit old places connected with your family if local, *eg* the church your parents got married in.

## Using secondary sources

The school and your local library are a great source of history books of all kinds. Younger children will enjoy stories about famous people, myths and legends and their family. Older children can enjoy reading about how and why things happened and how things in the past worked. One very popular series of books shows cut away pictures of how battleships, castles *etc* were created.

Young children have problems understanding time and the idea of past, present and future. In the younger age group (5 to 7) a lot of time is spent introducing children to the concept of the past through stories, visits, family history and constructing a timeline. At the older level teachers develop historical skills further.

At each level the teachers can choose a fixed number of topics from a set number suggested in the National Curriculum guidelines. There has been a lot of discussion about what topics should be included and how much recent history should be taught. But all the topics chosen will help children to develop their historical skills. These involve encouraging children to:

● remember names, dates, *etc*

● break the past into manageable parts

● use evidence to draw conclusions

● be aware that not all evidence can be trusted

● think and use common sense in reasoning.

History also combines naturally with not just art and geography but also drama, music and Information Technology (IT).

## Combining history and geography

History and geography are often combined in topic work at primary school. There are many natural common features of both subjects and they also combine naturally with many other subjects such as art and maths.

## USING LOCAL EXAMPLES

You do not have to go very far to help your child understand history and geography. The area you live in is full of useful and interesting places to visit and things to find out about. Has your locality got any of these:

- a church

- a town hall

- a library

- a park.

You can also use your house or flat, your street, the local shopping centre *etc*. Everything in your local environment can be used to encourage your child's interest in geography and history. Your child will find it all the more interesting because it relates to things that he or she knows well.

### Using a park

When you go to the local park you can ask your child questions? Where is the playground? Which is nearer, the duck pond or the bench we usually sit on? Which direction is the gate? Add some history questions – why do you think they built this park? Is it older than you? What is that building for? When you get home you can make a simple map of the park and help your child find out about the park's history – your library may have a booklet by the local council.

### Starting a history and geography scrapbook

You can help your child compile a scrapbook of source material for your local area. It will involve history and geography. Your child can put in pictures, photos and drawings of places you have visited, maps and plans he or she has drawn or bought, information from books and leaflets *etc*. It will be interesting and fun to compile and provide background information for school projects.

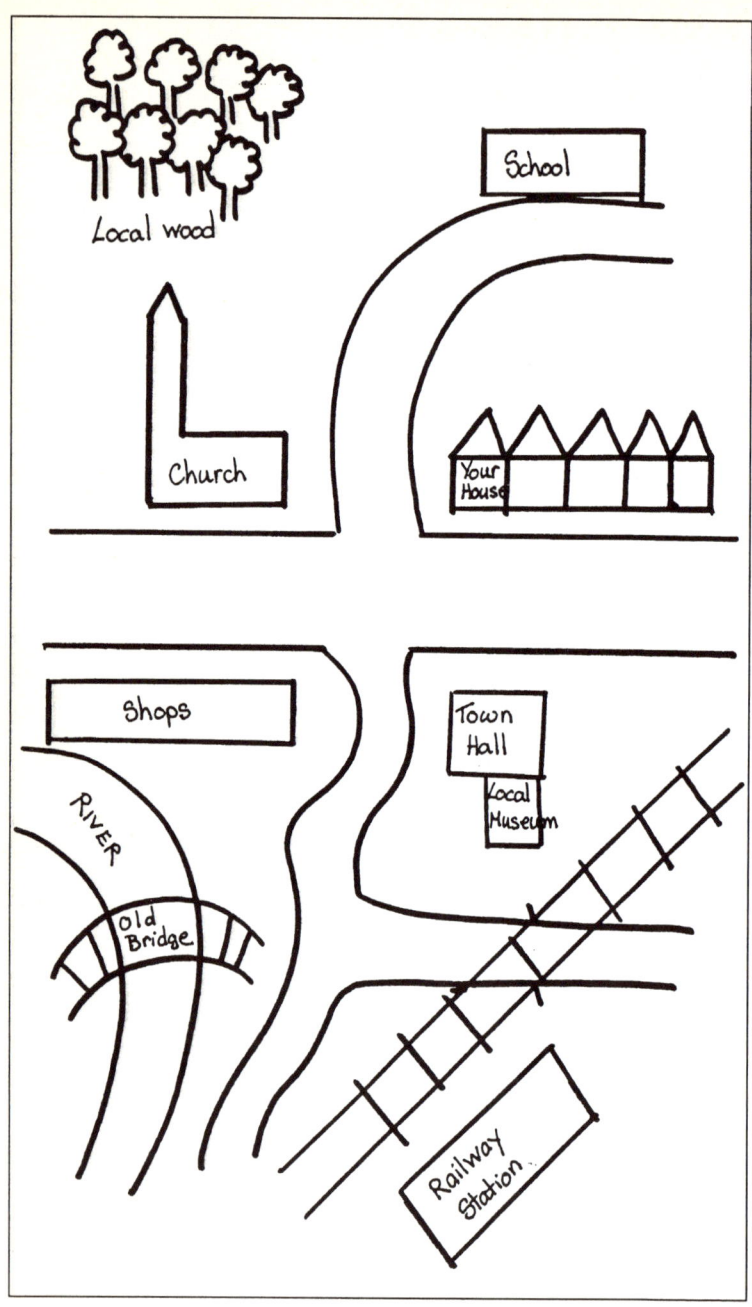

Fig. 7. Finding history and geography where you live.

## INVESTIGATING AND RECORDING

Both geography and history involve finding out and recording what you can see. They are not only important skills but are fun too. By making you and your child look carefully at the world around you will be seeing it in a new light and getting a better understanding of it.

### Investigating

Investigating means finding out about things. You can help your child do this by:

- taking your child on visits
- looking at local buildings
- choosing and using appropriate books
- looking for pictures and photos
- taking photos of people and places
- helping them draw pictures and maps
- making models
- making books
- helping them write descriptions of places.

### Learning to record

Both history and geography involve recording. This does not have to be very complicated and will get more sophisticated as children get older. So younger children can record by drawing pictures, taking photos, *etc.*

Older children can record by writing descriptions, taking photos, measuring, making models, making graphs *etc.* They can write their own descriptions and make a booklet of their work.

## QUESTIONS AND ANSWERS

*I don't know much about my family. How can I help my child with a family history project?*

Help your child draw a simple family tree of his or her immediate family. Find some photos of yourself as a child. Look for things you owned when younger – even some old records from your teenage years is part of history! If your relatives live far away help your child compose a tape or letter to send to them asking them about the family.

*I'm hopeless at map reading. How can I help my child with geography?*
Geography is not just about maps: it is also about the environment and how people live and work in other countries, the weather, *etc*. Use books and pictures to interest your child. Ask your child to explain maps to you! You will enjoy discovering the world together.

*My child's class is going on a trip to a local church. Is that history or geography?*
In primary school it is probably both. The history will be in finding out about the age of the church, what happened to it, who used it and why. The geography will be in finding out why it is there and its relationship to the town and other landmarks and what it is made of. Both will involve recording and discovery.

## PRACTISING BASIC RESEARCH SKILLS

Basic research skills include:

1. Researching.

2. Evaluating.

3. Recording.

### Researching

Research skills involve not just finding things out, but knowing where and how to do so. So, for example, your child will need to know that he or she can get information from books but will also need to know:

1. Where to find the right books.

2. How to use a book to extract information.

3. How to judge how useful a book iso.

4. How to judge how accurate a book is.

Your child will learn a lot of these skills at school. But you can help by showing your child how to find things out. You might take them to look at a building to find out what it looks like, then help them find a book which describes the style of building, then find a curator who can tell your child about the building and so on. Or you can walk to the park and then go to the library to find a map of the area showing the park.

## Evaluating

If you are reading a history or geography book, how accurate is it? Does it tell you what you want to know? Is it biased in any way? When looking at primary evidence what does it tell you about what you are interested in?

Primary children will not be able to do all these things but they can make a start. You can help them by encouraging them to ask questions abut the sources they use. Older children looking at an old newspaper article or a map, for example, can ask:

● Was it written at the time of the event it describes?

● Has it missed anything out?

● Is it presenting one view rather than another?

● Is it a modern or old map?

● Who made it and why?

● Does it show everything?

Encouraging your child to ask questions is an important part of helping your child with history and geography.

## Recording

Helping your child with recording skills can be great fun. Why not start with your own house? Even a modern house or flat had to be designed and built by someone. And it can be drawn, measured, looked up on a map.

Basic recording skills include:

● drawing pictures

● drawing maps and plans

● writing descriptions

● recording measurements, directions, designs

● taking photographs

● making notes from books.

## VISITING PLACES OF INTEREST

Visiting places of interest is a major part of introducing your child to geographic and historical skills. It is also great fun for both adults and children, as long as you don't try to make the visit too long or expect the child to take everything seriously. Many places of interest put on special programmes for children so you can find out about these. Other places might have playgrounds and picnic areas to give you and your child a break.

Don't try to take your child around all of a site or a museum. Pick a bit that might interest them and let them spend as long as they like looking at it. Talk to them about it, answer their questions (if you can) or ask an attendant to do so. Let them decide what they want to see.

If the visit is related to a school project the teacher will have already taken the children on a visit. You can take your child back on a later date to let them look at something in particular.

## Finding history and geography

There are many places you can take your child to help them appreciate history and geography. Remember that visits should be fun – don't expect your child to spend hours looking at furniture in a stately home or walking for hours around a town looking at buildings. It is better to make visits short and to look at one or two things in particular. You can always make another visit on another occasion.

Look in these places:

- museums

- art galleries

- English Heritage sites

- National Trust properties

- private stately homes

- archaeological sites

- churches/monasteries

- country parks

- your local town or village

- seaside

- local countryside.

Many of these places have special exhibitions or 'hands on' days for children or arrange special children's events to help them enjoy their visit as well as learn about the past. Modern technology has enabled some places to provide videotronic shows where models of people in the past are made to 'talk'. In the countryside and parks look for nature trails and information boards.

## FOLLOWING UP ENTHUSIASMS

Whether your child suddenly becomes interested in the Romans or Norwegians, the local church or how farms work, you can help them follow up their enthusiasm. Apart from books there are societies as well. For example, your local archaeology society might have a junior section or the local rambling club might encourage families with children to join them.

Also when you go to visit places there are often brochures, maps and plans for sale and sometimes free leaflets. Pick these up wherever you go so that your child can look at them later as well as while on the visit.

There are also fun things you can do together to foster an interest in the subjects. For example:

- going on country walks
- brass rubbing centres
- visits to archaeological digs
- finding information via computers
- watching film or videos about people and places.

## CASE STUDIES

### Geoff learns about his family

Sally notices that Geoff starts asking questions about this family. 'How old is granny? Where does Uncle Mike live?' She learns that Geoff's class is doing a project on 'the family'. The children have been asked to bring in pictures and objects connected with their families. Sally takes Geoff to visit granny. Granny tells him 'when I was a little girl I lived on a farm and my daddy, your great grandaddy, showed me how to milk the cows'. She gives Geoff a photo of herself aged ten with her brothers in front of the farmhouse. Together granny and Geoff draw a simple family tree. Geoff takes both the photo and family tree to school and his teacher puts them up on the wall.

### Becky's parents help her draw a map

Becky's class have been drawing a plan of the school. Becky likes looking at the plan and wants to draw one of her house. 'Show us how you did it at school', her parents suggest. Becky tells them how to pace out measurements and shows them what to do. She lets her parents pace out some measurements while she records them. Together they draw out the plan of the house and the garden. Becky is learning to explain things clearly. She is proud of the map and takes it to school to show her teacher.

### Harry takes Eddy and Mark to a museum

Harry is keen to help Mark and Eddy with their environmental studies. He decides to take them to the city museum which has a large section on Romans. He and this sons spend three hours there and look at all the exhibits. By the end of the afternoon both boys are cross, tired and hungry. 'What's up with you two? Didn't you like it?' asks Harry. 'But Dad', says Mark, 'I wanted to look at the Romans longer. I wanted to see what soldiers wore.' Harry realises that he has tried to pack too much in. The next month he takes them to the museum again. This time the boys each choose a section to look at. Harry gives them paper and pencils so they can draw their favourite bits. Mark draws a model Roman soldier in uniform. Eddy loses his paper but has a lovely time talking to an attendant about the pictures of prehistoric animals on the walls. They stay for an hour and a half – and Harry makes sure that they all have biscuits and a drink in the museum café before they go home!

### SUMMARY

- History and geography often overlap.

- Use your neighbourhood to look for local examples.

- Help your child practise basic research skills.

- Visit places of interest.

- Help your child follow up particular interests.

# 7

## Learning about Information Technology

Information Technology (IT) is now an important part of the National Curriculum. It involves learning how to use IT equipment and software, that is, computers and keyboards and the programs they need.

Children are not usually scared of IT. In fact, given guidance and suitable programs they often put adults to shame with their willingness to adapt to using the new technology.

The most important thing you can do for your child regarding IT is to enable them to gain familiarity with computers and related technology so that they are confident about using it.

### Learning to use IT

At primary level children learn to use a variety of IT equipment to:

● solve problems

● communicate

● handle information

● explore real and imaginary situations.

IT is also used across many subjects and will be used to:

● solve problems

● present information

● support learning

● understand how IT affects work and society

● contact other people (by e-mail or Internet).

## USING COMPUTER PROGRAMS

At school your child will use computers from a young age. Even reception age children are given the opportunity to use computers where they are available.

They can use computers for:

- maths

- English

- geography

- history

- art

and many other subjects.

Children need to use programs that are suitable for their age group. If the school provides suitable programs children rapidly increase in confidence and ability.

The same applies at home if you have a computer for your child to use. Provide programs suitable for their age and let them increase in complexity as they get older.

The equipment at both home and school needs to have suitable:

- hardware

- software.

## Choosing computer hardware

Computer **hardware** is the machinery that makes up a computer set-up. It usually consists of:

- computer base

- computer monitor

- keyboard

- disks.

It might also include:

- a modem (if not internal)

- speakers.

Computer hardware is connected together and is then connected to an electricity supply. To use the Internet it must have a modem and be connected to a phone line too.

*Affording IT*

You do not need to buy an expensive PC but it helps if it can use the same kind of software as the school does. Access to the Internet is important nowadays too. Ask at your local computer shop for a computer set up that does the basics – don't buy more fancy bits and pieces than you need. Try not to buy a computer with lots of games already installed.

## Choosing software

**Software** is the programs that you can store in your computer's memory to help it do things – such as play games, do word-processing, or access the Internet. Software is stored in the computer's main memory (the hard disk) or on diskettes or CDs. You can add programs by buying CDs or diskettes with programs on and following simple instructions to install them on your computer.

*Buying games and programs for a computer*
You might be tempted to buy lots of games for the computer but some will probably already be on it. These will vary from very simple children's games to complicated (and possibly unsuitable) adult games.

Before you decide what software to buy you need to decide what your child will need. Most computers will already have a word-processing program installed and perhaps a spreadsheet and games. This might sound adequate but if your child is just starting primary school they might need a very simple word-processing package or game to help them. Young children might also need:

- reading games
- maths games
- simple drawing program.

As they get older you could get them:

- spelling programs
- encyclopaedia
- more advanced maths programs/games
- design package
- language learning program.

Your choice of computer programs will be decided by the child's age and abilities and also by what the teacher recommends. Don't be afraid of asking what programs the teacher recommends for use at home. You want to complement and support IT work in the school.

spelling programs
maths games
language learning
encyclopaedias
drawing programs

Fig. 8. Computer programs for children's education.

## EDUCATION ON CDS

Most modern computers have a disk drive for CDs. This means that CDs with ROM (Read Only Memory) can be played and the information will appear on the computer screen. The capabilities of CDs are impressive. Not only can they show written information but also play sound, pictures and moving pictures.

One CD can hold many times the information of an ordinary computer disk and many volumes of books. The entire set of the *Encyclopaedia Britannica* is now on one CD.

This means that children using computers have access to a vast amount of knowledge available on CDs.

### Using CDs

CDs can be expensive so those containing vast amounts of information such as the *Britannica* are best left to schools and libraries to buy. There are less complicated versions of encyclopaedias designed especially for children and your school might use these. Some of these are American but the basic information is the same whether English or American.

There is no need for you to buy expensive information CDs but you can help your child by buying games CDs. These are less expensive and many are especially designed to help children's learning. For example, you can buy games on CDs to help with:

- maths

- English

- foreign language

- art.

Many computers have games already installed. Otherwise you need to play the CD each time or install a permanent version on the computer (the instructions will tell you how to do it).

*Getting information from CDs*
Because CDs can contain vast amounts of data they are very useful if your child needs to get information. Perhaps they become very interested in something and want to find out more about it. Or perhaps their teacher has asked them to find out something as part of their homework.

An encyclopaedic CD can provide all the information your child might need. The information can be printed out too. This is particularly useful if your child needs to find pictures to include in a piece of work.

Books will not be replaced by the information on computers and you should encourage your child to look at the relevant books too.

## Using computers at the library
Not everyone has a computer at home so more and more libraries are providing computers for their users. These might have many uses:

- library catalogue

- job information

- courses information

- Internet access

- word processing.

In the children's library they might also have some simple educational games for children.

The jobs and courses information will not interest your child but you can help them use the library catalogue. Most libraries have their information on a computer nowadays so learning how to use it in your local library will help your child in any library.

The word processing is useful to help your child type and print out work – perhaps homework for school.

Most libraries will ask you to book time on their computer so that everyone gets a fair go. The librarian will show your child how to use the computer and be around to help if they have a problem. You can learn too – in fact many parents have conquered their fear of computers by learning about them with their children!

*Using the library catalogue*
The library catalogue will be easy to use but you can always ask the librarian to show you and your child how to use it. Sometimes your child will have to use the mouse to move a cursor around the screen; sometimes simply press certain keys. The information on the screen will tell you how to find a book by author, subject or title.

*Getting to the Internet*
The library will probably already be connected to the Internet so it will be easy for you and your child to use. Ask the librarian to show you what to do. You can use search systems to find information on subjects you choose.

*Using e-mail*
You are less likely to find e-mail in use for the public at a library. But even if it is not available the librarian can tell you how to use it. Some schools are now providing each child with an e-mail address. This means that when they access a particular part of the computer they can send and receive messages from other people. Teachers can use it to write to their pupils too.

*Using word processing*
Most libraries with computers will offer word processing. This means that your child can type the words onto the computer screen using the computer keyboard and then check the spelling and the way the page looks before printing it out.

## DISCOVERING THE INTERNET

The Internet is really a way of connecting millions of computers all over the world. You can access the Internet and then obtain information from other computers. The amount of information available is vast. Some of it is also unsuitable for children. If your child uses the Internet at school the school will have made sure that certain sites cannot be contacted. You can do the same on a home computer by using a program that allows you to decide what kind of sites your child can look at.

Using search engines helps your child to find the information they are looking for. A word, perhaps 'elephant' is typed in and the computer then provides a list of all the sites it can find that have information about elephants. Some will be very useful; others not at all. Not all the information is good quality because, unlike books, there is nothing to stop anyone putting out any information they like. So a lot of it is only opinion, not established fact. You can sometimes judge the quality of the information by the name of the person or organisation that is providing it. So if information about elephants was provided by London Zoo you could trust it to be accurate and up-to-date. If it was provided by a Mr Smith of Australia perhaps less so.

Information and pictures from the Internet can be printed out too. But you must make sure that your child does not pretend it is his or her own work. They can use the information in it to write their own words or they can write that the piece of paper was copied from the Internet so that their teacher knows which is the child's own work.

*Hunting for 'elephants'*
To give your child practice with using the Internet play the 'elephant' game. Give your child a list of five words and ask them to find five different facts about each word using the Internet. Use nouns and names of famous people.

## USING E-MAIL

E-mail is a way of sending and receiving letters by using a computer and a telephone line. You or your school need to have bought access to the Internet from one of the many Internet providers. They provide e-mail facilities with their Internet package. Your child will have his or her own e-mail address and can then communicate with other people across the world, *eg* pupils in other schools or relatives.

Some schools give each child an e-mail address so that they can do this. If you have a computer at home your child might have to use your e-mail address unless your provider can arrange for several addresses. Other written work and pictures can be sent by e-mail too.

## Real-time discussion

This is a way of 'talking' by computer. Your child can type in a sentence and the person on another computer can type a reply which appears on your child's screen. Some people have this facility on their home computer but it's more likely to be used in schools so that older pupils can talk to other pupils across the world.

*Real time dangers*

There are real dangers in allowing your child to talk to strangers via a computer. The people at the other end might be:

● disguising their true identity

● disguising their age or sex

● trying to exploit children

● trying to involve children in pornography.

At school your child will be protected by the security measures that the school takes regarding the sites pupils can log into. Teachers will be vigilant too and keep an eye on what appears on the school computer screens and whom the children talk to. If real time talking is used children will normally be in contact with pupils in other schools known to the teachers.

In the home you can use commercial security software to block entry to certain kinds of Internet sites. You should also make sure that your child understands the basic **safety rules** of using a computer to contact other people:

1. Never give your full name and address to anyone over the Internet or by e-mail.

2. If the language or pictures become rude or unpleasant stop immediately and tell a teacher or parent.

3. Never arrange to meet anyone you have contacted via a computer.

As a parent your best guard against computer danger is to share the experience with your child. This is especially important when they are young and are learning how to use it. As they get older popping in to keep an eye on what they are doing is important and also gives you a chance to talk to them about what they are doing.

## MONITORING YOUR CHILD'S COMPUTER LEARNING

You may wonder how long to let your child sit at a computer or play computer games or use the Internet. There have been lots of stories about children turning into computer zombies. Don't worry, your child is unlikely to do that!

You can monitor your child's computer learning in several ways:

1. Provide computer games suitable for their age.

2. Put a safeguard on access to Internet sites.

3. Limit the time spent on the computer, *eg* an hour each evening; an hour and a half at weekends.

4. Encourage your child to use a computer for productive work, *eg* finding information or doing schoolwork.

5. Limit the use of computer games with no educational content to 'rewards' at certain times.

### Asking the teacher

Your child's teacher is the best person to ask about what computer activities are suitable for your child's age and abilities. The teacher can tell you what you can do to supplement what the child does at school. For example, he might suggest that your child uses a particular type of maths game or program so that they can practise what has been done in the classroom, or that they use spelling games to improve their vocabulary and spelling.

### USING TELEVISION AND VIDEO

Although not strictly IT, television and videos are included here because they are technological equipment much used in schools. There are many good educational and information programmes made for TV and video and schools find them useful to supplement standard class work.

You and your child can share the experience of TV and videos together. It is always tempting to leave children unattended in front of the TV and sometimes this will do no harm. But to get the best out of TV you need to do a number of things:

1. Choose programmes for your child to watch with you and on their own.

2. Limit the time in front of the TV.

3. Try to watch TV or videos with your child so that you can talk about them or answer questions.

4. Follow up interesting TV or video programmes.

## Choosing a programme/video

TV listings in newspapers and magazines tell you when educational programmes are on. If these are at an unsuitable time and you have a video you can record them to watch with your child at a later date. Other TV programmes are often interesting and relevant to your child's school work, for example:

● nature programmes

● history progammes

● travel documentaries

● science programmes

● language programmes.

Videos too come in many varieties which can be useful to your child. You do not have to buy them because your local library probably has a video collection from which you can borrow. It will have videos suitable for children as well as adults. The range of videos includes the kinds mentioned above for TV programmes but also includes:

● hobbies

● sports

● films not shown on TV.

Do not deprive your children of non-educational videos or TV. Some of it is entertaining and informative and everyone needs to have some fun!

## Limiting the time in front of the TV or video

Nowadays it is recognised that it is unhealthy for children to spend all their spare time sitting in front of the TV screen. You will help them do better at primary school by limiting the time your child watches TV or videos. Be firm about the time limit and perhaps extend it as a reward for good behaviour. It is better for your child to do other things such as play games or a sport or persue an interest or hobby or read books.

## Watching with your child

You cannot spend all your time watching TV with your child. But you should try to watch some programmes or videos with them. That way you can monitor what is suitable and be there to answer questions. You can talk about what you are watching: this gives your child the opportunity to learn to evaluate good and bad programmes and to learn how to extract information or opinions from them. By seeing how you react your child will learn which kind of programmes and videos have value.

Sharing an entertainment programme or video for pleasure is valuable too because it gives you and your child an experience in common and brings you closer together.

## Following up interests from TV or videos

Seeing something on TV or a video can make a subject seem vivid and exciting. Your child might well want to find out more about something they have seen. This is one reason why you should try to view with your child so that you can understand what they are interested in.

Programmes and films can be followed up by looking up more information in books or visiting places seen on the screen.

The process works the other way too. If your child becomes interested in something it is often possible to find a video or a TV programme that is relevant. You can then arrange to watch it together to see what it adds to your knowledge of the subject.

*Using videos*
Much of what applies to TV also applies to videos, but they do have some additional advantages. You can:

● record programmes from the TV to play later

● make a collection of videos on a particular subject

● exchange videos with other people.

## QUESTIONS AND ANSWERS

*Is it all right for my child to hand in printed homework?*
Unless the teacher has specifically asked for homework to be written by hand to practise handwriting, it is usually okay for your child to hand in printed work. As your child gets older he or she will find that the teacher sometimes specifically asks for work to be typed into a computer and printed out and will allow time in class for pupils to do this. If in any doubt ask the teacher.

*Should my child learn to type?*
Learning to use a keyboard correctly is very useful, but it is not important for young children to be able to touch type. Children need to get used to where the letters and numbers are on a keyboard. Older

children might like to try a computer 'teach yourself touch-typing' program for fun.

*Is using IT equipment dangerous?*
No – your child is quite safe. However, it is not sensible to let your child spend hours in front of the computer if only because they should be doing a variety of things.

## CASE STUDIES

### Sally and Geoff watch TV together

Geoff likes watching TV and if allowed will happily spend hours in front of it each evening. Sally does not want Geoff to become lazy so she limits his viewing to an hour each evening. She tries to watch with Geoff so that she can share his experiences. One day Geoff says 'Why can't I watch late like my friends?' Sally doesn't want Geoff to watch programmes late but doesn't want to prevent him sharing experiences with his peers. She decides to let him watch a later programme on a Saturday night but only if she watches it too and he goes straight to bed afterwards.

### Becky finds an interesting site

Becky is getting more confident about using the computer which pleases her parents. She can even use the Internet with a little help. But one day she runs to her parents in tears. She has logged onto an Internet site showing 'rude' pictures. Her parents are horrified but realise that it is partly their fault for not taking more care about what Becky can see. They ban using the computer until they have bought a software program that 'locks away' certain kinds of unsuitable sites. Her father sits next to her the next time Becky uses the computer and shows her that most sites are okay – even boring! He explains that now she can't get to any 'rude' sites even by accident. Becky regains her confidence and with her father's help finds a site about elephants to help with her latest school project.

### Eddy and Mark get a video from Uncle Joe

Uncle Joe lives in Australia and the boys miss him. One day they get a packet in the post. It is a video from Uncle Joe. It shows him talking about life in Australia and film of animals and different places in Australia that Uncle Joe has visited. It also has film of Aunty Sally and their cousins Billy and Ella. The boys love the film and it is informative too. They can see what makes Australia different – Harry and the boys have a lot to talk about. 'Can we make a video to send back?' the boys ask. Harry borrows a video camera from a friend and helps the boys to make their own film to send to Uncle Joe. They learn a lot about working a video camera. The experience is a great success and Mark writes about it for this school diary. Eddy tells his class about Australian animals when they do a project on animals in hot countries.

## SUMMARY

- Choose computer programs that are appropriate for your child's age and abilities.

- If you haven't got a computer use one at the local library.

- Help your child to use the Internet.

- Tell your child not give their personal details to anyone over the Internet.

- Watch TV and videos with your child and talk about them.

- Keep an eye on what your child watches and uses.

# 8

## Experiencing Art, Design and Music

This chapter deals with art and crafts, design and technology, and music.

### Using art

Art helps children:

- develop perception
- develop aesthetic judgement
- value and experience their own and others' cultural heritage, past and present
- develop a particular interest or aptitude.

In doing art they will learn about:

- form
- colour
- objects and materials

and will do so through:

- drawing
- painting
- making models
- construction.

### THINKING ABOUT ART AND CRAFTS

At school your child will be given opportunities to experience different approaches to art, craft and design. He or she will learn different ways in which ideas, feelings and meanings are communicated through art.

You probably think first of drawing and painting when you think of art. But art involves much more than this. Think about:

- making models

- computer art

- pottery

- performance art

- printing

- sculpture.

There is much in the world around us that is art. By experiencing art your child will learn to:

- express ideas and feelings

- record observations

- design and make images and objects

- learn skills, techniques and use of tools

- discover the work of different kinds of artist and craftspeople.

## Preparing for art and crafts

You need somewhere to work and a flat surface to work on. It could be an easel, a table, a stool, a piece of strong cardboard, an off-cut of wood, or even the floor.

Where you and your child will do your art will depend on where you live and what is available. Possibilities include the kitchen table or floor, or outside on a sunny day in the yard or the garden.

Whatever you do make sure that your child is well covered up if he or she is going to be doing something messy with paints, clay or glue, for example. Also, if they are going to be using anything sharp or potentially dangerous like scissors you will need to supervise them.

Make sure that what you give them to use is appropriate. Younger children will need larger pots, brushes, scissors *etc* than older children because they need equipment which is easy to handle. Also fit the medium to the child. Giving fine brushes and water-colour paints to a six year old will mean your child ends up dissatisfied because the result will be unsatisfactory.

## DRAWING, PAINTING AND CRAFT WORK

Drawing, painting and crafts cover many different types of use of equipment and skills. Here are some examples:

- finger painting

- using pens/pencils/crayons/paints

- collages

- clay models

- lino cuts

- sewing.

All these come under the heading of art and crafts – even making collages, which is really painting or drawing with paper.

Your child will try out most of these at school but there is nothing to stop you doing it at home too. It will not be the same and will help your child practise the skills he or she is learning at school. You get a chance to try too!

## Providing the right equipment

Make sure that any area you use for art or craft is covered with lots of newspaper to keep the mess in one place. Provide your child with an apron or adult shirt to keep them clean. Dress them in washable clothes, ones that you don't mind them getting dirty. If you can let your child work outside the mess won't matter so much and they will enjoy the feeling of freedom it gives them. If you will be helping them you should be similarly attired.

Use large pieces of paper where possible so that your child can draw or paint without restriction. Paper can be expensive but you can use:

- large envelopes cut open on three sides

- the backs of circulars

- the back of old bits of wallpaper, or lining paper

- brown wrapping paper.

## Art and craft ideas

You will probably find that your child is full of ideas. But if your child does ask you 'what shall I do?' suggest one of these:

- draw a favourite story or song

- make a puppet

- use potatoes for printing

- make a model out of plasticine or old boxes.

*Making a collage picture*
Collage is really painting with paper. Get lots of old magazines, cards, brochures and newspapers. Provide your child with scissors of a suitable size and a simple glue such as water and flour glue (water and flour mixed to a paste) or a glue stick and ask them to make a picture by cutting up the papers and sticking them on a large sheet. Your child could make a pattern or a picture with cut or torn pieces of paper. For something different suggest they decorate a shoe box or a scrapbook cover.

## CREATING WITH DESIGN AND TECHNOLOGY

Design and technology is closely linked to art and craft work. It combines design and making skills to create products. Children use knowledge and understanding of tools, materials and techniques to produce a finished product. Think of Blue Peter models and you get the idea!

### Putting design and technology to work

Design and technology starts by posing problems. Encourage your children to ask questions about how things work. Look at a bridge, for example. You could ask: Why was that bridge built there? Why was it built of that? How was it built? What would happen if it was built of something else? Is there a better way of building a bridge?

Once your child has posed a problem you can start to help him or her try to solve it. There are four stages to design:

1. Identify a need, *eg* a better bridge?

2. Create a design.

3. Plan and make a model.

4. Evaluate the result.

Construction kits such as Meccano or Lego are good for trying out designs. Older children can use the technical versions to make moving models. Moving parts can also be made using, for example, string to make simple cranes, rubber bands twisted to move parts as they unwind, *etc.* Part of the experience of design and technology is discovering the properties of materials and using them to make working models.

*Making a puppet*
Making a puppet is a fun design and technology project. Depending on the age of the child you can make a puppet from:

- egg boxes

- material – draw a simple shape with body, arms and head on two pieces of material and sew together

- *papier mâché* – make a *papier mâché* head and glue it to a sewn body

- an old sock – stuff the toe with old material, tie round the neck

- card and string.

*Drawing a design board*

Before your child starts making a model get them to draw six large squares on a piece of paper or card. Explain that they need to show how they are going to make the model in six stages. Compare the pictures with the finished product.


## MAKING MUSIC

Music is an active experience with three main parts:

1. Composing.

2. Performing.

3. Listening.

All three of these are the basis of good musicianship. But above all music is and should be fun. It is something that you and your child can enjoy together.

You do not need to be able to play an instrument or know a lot about music to help your child enjoy it. You can learn about music with your child and through music help him or her grow.

Your child's primary school might be lucky enough to have a specialist music teacher but most music is taught by the class teacher. Most of them are not music specialists but will be giving as much help and practice with music as they can. You can help support their efforts at home.

### Understanding music

Music is a creative process that simultaneously uses two or three of the three basic activities of composing, performing and listening. For example, your child could listen and clap in time to a beat, or try out ideas for tunes (composing) by performing them.

composing → performing → listening

You don't have to start with any one part of the process in particular. You can start anywhere and introduce your child to other aspects later. The main thing is that it is fun.

## Composing

Children often make up their own songs and tunes. If they have access to instruments they might pick out sounds on them or they can use their voices. Your child's voice is a musical instrument too – and more portable than most! But there are ways of finding instruments around the home.

*Finding instruments at home*
Try these home-made instruments:

● milk bottles filled with different levels of water and hit with a pencil

● upturned tin cans hit with a spoon

● dried peas or lentils sealed in a tin or box and rattled.

*Using cheap instruments*
You do not have to have a piano or any other main orchestral instrument to encourage your child to make music. Some instruments are comparatively cheap to buy – even the toy version can give some pleasure. If you can't afford them or can't find them perhaps you could borrow them from a friend:

● recorder

● triangle

● tambourine

● mouth organ

● tin whistle

● small xylophone.

## Helping your child to compose music

If your child does not naturally try to make up tunes or songs you can encourage them in various ways. Try asking them to make up a new version of a familiar song or to make up a tune to a poem or story. The tune could be hummed or la-laed. You could then try to copy it.

When they are making sounds on their instrument or with their voice you can show them simple ways of writing their music down:

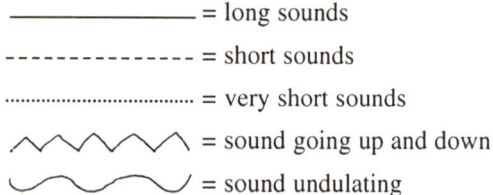

= long sounds

= short sounds

= very short sounds

= sound going up and down

= sound undulating

Ask your child to make up their own symbols for different sounds. For example, ask them how they would draw 'loud' or 'slow'.

## Using musical language

You might not use musical language when talking to your child about music. But you should understand what the terms mean. As you and your child make music together you should encourage your child to recognise:

- pitch – whether a sound is high or low

- duration – how long a beat or rhythm lasts: is it long or short?

- dynamics – whether a sound is loud or soft or whether there is silence

- tempo – the speed of the music

- timbre – the kind of sound, *eg* smooth, rough, rattling

- texture – sounds played together or alone

- structure – beginning, middle, end.

*Playing a composing game*
Using the symbols your child has designed draw them out on a pack of plain postcards or about 20 pieces of paper. Draw several copies of each symbol. Your child can either use his or her voice to make sounds or you can use one of the home instruments suggested above. Place the cards face down on a table. Ask your child to choose three cards and to play what they say. For example, suppose your child had picked cards with symbols for a long sound, going down, sounding 'wiggly'. They can then sing or play that sound for you. Of course, on some of the instruments they won't be able to play all three parts of the sound and you can talk to them about why not.

## Performing

Singing or playing music is a basic part of learning about music. It is naturally a part of most children's lives as they listen to music on CDs, tapes, the radio and TV. They often sing along and dance to the music too. This all helps to improve their sense of rhythm. Listening to music and singing together is great fun. Don't worry if your voice is not 'perfect'. As long as the tune is recognisable and you are enjoying it, your child won't worry. And by listening to your child you will improve your own ability to make music.

Making musical sounds at home is enjoyable too. Especially if you play one instrument, your child another and you both sing – you have a group!

## Finding songs to sing and play

Children will enjoy the kinds of songs listed below. All are easy to find in books in the shops or library. Or your child could borrow a song book from school with the teacher's help:

● alphabet and counting songs, *eg* 'ten green bottles' or 'one man went to mow'

● nursery songs

● pop songs

● traditional folk songs and ballads

● songs from other lands and cultures

● seasonal songs.

As they get older they can also try:

● rounds, *ie* one person starts singing, another starts the song a little later, *eg* 'London's burning' is often sung as a simple round

● simple part songs.

Of course, not all songs are suitable for all ages. Rounds will be beyond young children and some traditional folk songs can be quite difficult to understand and sing. But as your child gets older you can introduce them to a variety of musical experiences. Don't neglect the simple songs as your child gets older. Children still enjoy nursery rhymes long after nursery age.

## Encouraging performance

Encourage your child to be active when making music. Ask them to sing and clap to music and songs. Ask them to sing you a song so that you can repeat it. Sing with your child.

Play one of the home instruments while your child plays another. Sing a song as you play the tune or beat time. Ask your child to sing you the songs he or she learns in the school playground. You might be surprised to find that many are the same ones you sung in the playground when you were young.

### Reading music

Your child does not need to be able to read music, that is to understand the notes of music as formally written out. Neither do you. It is possible to learn to understand and enjoy music without this. In fact most primary schools do not teach it automatically. If an individual child seems ready to understand it their teacher might start to show them how it works.

At home you can show your child the music notation in song books, just as children who can't read are shown books so that they get used to them.

### Performing for others

Music can be enjoyed alone or with others. One of the pleasure of music is to share it with other people. Your child can sing or play to friends or relatives: you can join in. Encourage the audience to join in too – that way your child will understand that music is for everyone.

## Listening

Listening to music helps concentration and this is something that is useful in other subjects. It also teaches your child to discriminate between:

● different sounds

● good and bad music

● music they like or don't like.

## Finding music to listen to

Music is all around us every day. Your child can hear music from:

● tapes of words with music

● tapes of songs and tunes

● CDs

- radio
- TV
- cinema
- in shops
- school assemblies.

Popular tapes for young children often have an accompanying book so that your child can sing along and look at the words and music at the same time. Younger children will obviously need your help to do this.

*Listening actively*
Listening actively is important. Don't just sit your child near a tape recorder or the radio and leave them. Ask them to listen carefully to the music. Can they describe the kind of sounds they are hearing? Use these words:

- high/low
- loud/soft
- fast/slow.

Ask them to use their own words to describe sounds. So they might come out with words like warm, bright, creaky, rustly. Never mind if *you* can't hear the sounds like that. It is the fact that your child is listening carefully and trying to describe accurately what they hear that is important.

## Listening to live music
Children respond more immediately to live music. Take any chance you can to hear music performed live: bands in the local park, a friend who can play an instrument, street performers, any one who is playing or singing in front of you.

It is important that you listen to music together. Apart from increasing pleasure your child needs to learn the etiquette of public listening, *eg* when to clap, when to join in.

## LEARNING AN INSTRUMENT

Many parents think that their child ought to be learning a traditional instrument in primary school and that their child is missing out unless they do so.

But apart from the fact that instrumental instruction is not available in many primary schools and that private tuition is expensive, learning an instrument is not necessarily important at that age:

If your child's primary school is one of the lucky ones that can offer instrumental tuition it might well be in an instrument such as the recorder or guitar. These instruments make nice noises fairly quickly and so, in theory, encourage children to continue playing.

Regular attendance at lessons and practice is important so do not encourage a child into learning an instrument unless you are confident they will want to continue. Remember that it can take a long time to play to a level reasonable enough to get enjoyment from a traditional instrument such as a violin.

If your child shows an interest in learning let him or her get to know instruments before choosing one. Perhaps a friendly music shop will let your child try some instruments or a friend will show your child one that they play.

*Playing instruments for children with disabilities*
Nowadays disabilities are no bar to musical skill. Children can be helped to play recorders and other basic instruments – some have even been especially adapted such as a one-handed recorder. Electronic instruments have opened up music to many children who are physically disabled.

Hearing disability too is no bar – think of Beethoven. There are professional musicians today who have overcome hearing disabilities.

Children with other special needs such as mental disability often greatly appreciate music and are enthusiastic performers and participants. Specially trained music teachers help these children to take part in music.

*Helping musically able children*
You are likely to know that your child is musically able by the way they question and talk about music and their general musical ability. They are among the ones who might benefit from learning an instrument and starting to understand musical notation. But don't push them. They will let you know in their own time what they want.

## QUESTIONS AND ANSWERS

*Is pop music bad for my child?*
Pop music is fun and does your child no harm. It teaches rhythm and

a sense of tune. You might not like it but remember that everyone has different tastes in music. If you listen you might even enjoy some of it.

*Is it all right to help my child make models?*
Yes, do help your child, but don't make the model for him or her. Help to collect the necessary materials and ask questions to help your child work out what they want to do. Try to let your child do as much of the actual construction as possible. Even if it doesn't look neat it will have taught them a lot.

*My child is learning the guitar. What kind should I buy?*
If your child is not lent a guitar by the school ask your local music shop whether they hire out instruments. That way your child can try it out without having to buy it. Many instruments come in smaller sizes suitable for children so you can get, for example, a three quarter size guitar or a quarter size violin. Ask your child's music teacher to recommend an instrument.

## CASE STUDIES

### Geoff and Sally sing songs
Geoff's school has been teaching the children to sing 'London's burning'. Geoff loves the song and is driving Sally crazy by singing it all the time. 'Why don't we try doing it a different way?' she asks one day. She helps Geoff make a 'drum kit' with some old boxes and spoons. 'We'll both sing' she says, 'and you can beat the time for us'. Geoff gets the hang of it quickly and they both sing the song several times. Geoff quickly gets used to playing the beat. Sally asks him to play the beat to other songs they both know. She finds some dry beans and puts them in a tin and rattles them in time to the songs. Geoff is pleased to have his own 'group'. 'Can I ask my friends to play?' he asks. Sally asks her friend Julie to bring her two children round. Geoff organises them into a group and they sing songs loudly all afternoon. Sally and Julie retreat to the kitchen for a cup of coffee and a bit of peace!

### Becky asks to learn the recorder
Becky enjoys music at her school. The school employs a specialist music teacher who takes each class once a week. Her class teacher also introduces music into the normal lessons. Becky wants to learn to play

the recorder. 'I will practise' she promises. The school can lend Becky a recorder for a few weeks to see if she likes it. Becky takes it seriously and Robert and Mary buy her a recorder after first asking the music teacher where to get it. 'Can I read the music too?' Becky asks. The teacher promises that she will learn the music notation as she learns the recorder. Becky starts her recorder lessons and is soon playing simple tunes.

## Harry introduces Mark and Eddy to older music

Neither Mark nor Eddy is particularly interested in music although they like singing along to the latest pop songs on the radio. Harry is a folk music enthusiast. One Saturday when Eddy is staying with friends Harry tells Mark 'I'm going to take you somewhere special this afternoon'. He takes Mark to a folk music festival in the local park. Mark enjoys the crowds but is not impressed by the music. But he is fascinated by seeing guitars played and by how loud live music is. Harry introduces Mark to his friend James who plays a guitar in one of the folk bands. James lets Mark hold his guitar and shows him how to play a chord. Mark returns from the festival determined to find a guitar – but preferably an electric one. Harry promises to buy a second hand electric guitar for Mark when he is twelve if he learns the basics on an ordinary guitar at school.

## SUMMARY

- Provide a suitable area for arts and crafts – and washable clothing!

- Use a variety of materials.

- Try some of the activities yourself.

- Sing and play music with your child.

- Do not force your child to learn a traditional instrument.

# 9

## Enjoying Sport

Sport is healthy and enjoyable. Children at primary school get the opportunity to take part in a wide range of physical activities suitable to their age and abilities.

At Key Stage 1 children are taught:

- games

- gymnastic activities

- dance.

At Key Stage 2 they also take part in:

- athletic activities

- outdoor and adventurous activities

- swimming.

Teachers in primary schools now have a wide range of discretion about what areas of PE are taught. Schools which previously spent time on outdoor and adventurous activities might choose to drop them and spend more time on swimming, games, dance and gymnastics.

Swimming still has a protected place in the National Curriculum because it is vital to children's safety to be able to swim. All children should be able to swim 25 metres by the time they leave primary school at the age of 11.

You might also find that your child's school chooses to combine some aspects of PE with other subjects. For example, it might combine dance and music lessons.

However your child's school chooses to organise its PE lessons your child will have regular swimming lessons and other forms of physical education, depending on the school's priorities and time-table.

### Learning new skills
Children enjoy learning new skills and finding out what their bodies can

do. Sport should be fun so that children are encouraged to stay physically fit throughout their lives. They therefore need to learn:

- to be physically active
- to make the best use of their bodies
- to take part in a wide range of physical activities.

Much sport involves co-operating with others, so children need to learn to:

- learn fair play
- cope with success and limitations
- look out for others
- try to improve their own performance.

*Being aware of safety*
When you are helping your child with sport remember that he or she needs to learn how to take part safely. Help them to:

- understand and follow instructions and rules
- wear appropriate clothing
- warm up before and cool down after vigorous physical activity.

## FINDING A SPORT YOUR CHILD ENJOYS

In primary schools the emphasis tends to be on physical activities that everyone can join in, such as gymnastics, dance or games. Where teams are involved such as rounders or football the emphasis is on taking part and enjoying the game rather than gloating over a win. Swimming is not only good for health but is an activity that can be enjoyed by everyone whatever the level of their ability. It is also enjoyed by children who prefer not to be part of team games.

### Learning what PE your child likes

Your child will probably make it clear quite early on what kind of physical activity he or she enjoys. If he or she constantly asks you to take them swimming or spends all his or her spare time playing football with friends, you will have a good idea!

Finding out what kind of physical activity appeals to them can be a matter of trial and error. There are many activities that you could try together until you find one that your child really enjoys. For example:

- swimming

- walking

- throwing a ball or a frisbee

- kicking a ball

- hitting a ball with a bat

- cycling

- orienteering

- ice-skating

- skateboarding

- table tennis

- skittles

- skipping

- dancing

- exercises.

Your child won't like everything you try together but it is important to give them the opportunity to experience as many different physical activities as possible so that they get to know what they prefer and are good at.

## Helping your child choose

Try activities together. For example, take your child swimming (try to find when the comparatively quiet times at your local pool are) and help them in the water. Throw a frisbee or ball for your child to catch. Kick a ball around in the park with them. Go cycling together. Borrow some light rackets (many shops sell plastic ones) and hit a soft ball for your child to return.

If you do any kind of activity yourself such as dancing, yoga or sailing, you could find out whether your child can try it. Perhaps the class and club you go to runs an open day or will let your child try it before or after the end of the usual session.

## Making activities fun

While you are helping your child to find out what he or she likes the school will be helping him or her take part in organised PE.

Encourage your child to take part in all the PE offered even if they

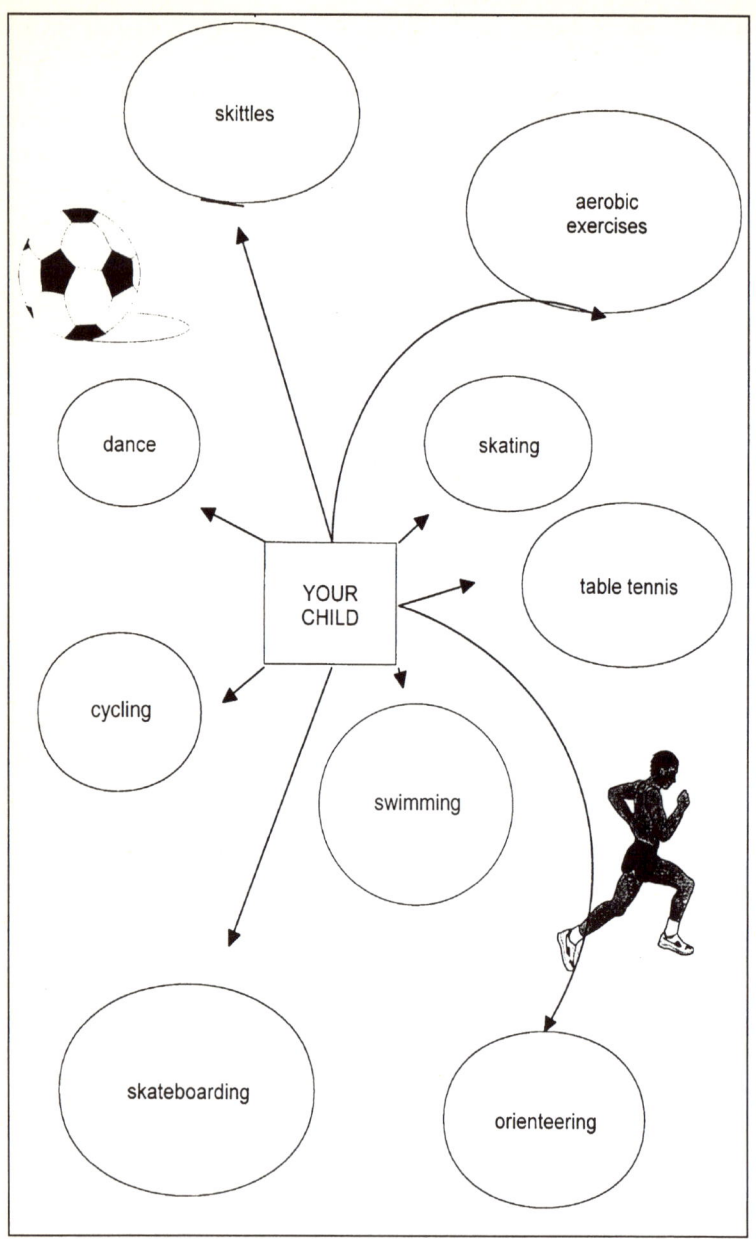

Fig. 9. Sport for all.

don't particularly like it. Regular physical activity is vital for good health and too many children nowadays do not do enough to stay healthy.

If the teacher mentions that your child really dislikes an activity and refuses to join in, talk to your child about it. Is there a particular problem that could be solved to make PE more acceptable to them? For example:

● Are your child's PE clothes different from the other children's?

● Is he or she fat and gets laughed at?

● Is your child not very good at the activity?

● Has your child hurt him or herself during the activity?

● Is the teacher very strict?

*Wearing different clothes*
One parent sent his child to PE at primary school with plimsolls for several weeks running. It was only later that he learnt that his child's reluctance to do PE was because all the other children were wearing trainers. A hastily bought pair of trainers solved the problem.

If your child complains that he or she is not wearing what other children do for PE this is one occasion when it is sensible to take notice. Ask other mothers what their children wear; ask the teacher what the children wear. It could be something as simple as a different coloured T-shirt – but it could make the difference between your child enjoying PE or not.

*Realising your child is fat*
It is hard for many parents to accept that their child might be fat. But obesity is a serious problem among even primary aged children and you should take it seriously.

If you do not notice your child's weight problem the school doctor or your child's teacher will undoubtedly gently point it out to you. You will probably have had some idea from your child's reluctance to go to PE lessons and complaints that the other children 'laugh at me 'cos I'm fat'. Don't dismiss this. The teacher will encourage your child to continue to take part in PE lessons because it is good for their health. He or she will take steps to stop name-calling.

You must do your part by making your child aware that you are taking the problem seriously. Start with straightforward things such as not letting them eat or drink sweet things between meals and by serving healthy food at teatime. Send them out with a good breakfast but don't let them snack. Ask your child's doctor for advice about diet and exercise to help get your child's weight down and make sure your child sticks to the advice.

Take your child out with you and encourage them to join with you in healthy activities – perhaps as suggested above. This will show the child that you take exercise seriously too. As the child's weight improves so will his or her self-confidence and enjoyment of PE.

An activity such as swimming is often enjoyed by fat children because their weight is not so obvious in the water and they do not risk letting a team down.

*Being no good at the activity*

Perhaps your child simply isn't any good at the activities the school encourages (although there is usually something that a child can manage) . Explain to your child that nobody is good at everything – in fact you are very bad at (name a sport you don't excel at). Encourage them to join in anyway 'for the fun' and help them find an activity out of school that they can enjoy without worrying whether they will be seen by their friends.

*Being hurt*

If your child gets hurt during games lessons it might put him or her off sport. Even if the injury is very minor, perhaps a bruised knee, it can be upsetting.

Encourage your child to take part in games lessons again as soon as possible. If he or she is still reluctant then take them to the park and play simple games such as catch or racing with them until they regain their confidence. Enlist the teacher's help too. It is not good for children to miss activity lessons.

## ENCOURAGING TALENT WITHOUT PRESSURE

Occasionally a child will be so good at sport that parents wonder whether they should encourage them to start professional training.

At primary school age it is rarely a good idea unless the child is so evidently talented that it is obvious to all. Even then it must be the child's wish, not the parents. If your child wants to do a lot more of a particular sport, perhaps swimming or football, then an out of school lesson once a week can do no harm. But putting young children into professional training routines involving hours of practice every day as well as competitions can be harmful.

Ask your child's teacher what they think. The school itself might run an after school club for, gymnastics or swimming, for example, so that your child can get extra enjoyment without undue pressure.

If your child wants to stop extra lessons, let them. It is better to let your child enjoy sport rather than put them off for life by forcing them to do it.

### Following your child's dreams not yours

Be careful not to confuse your desires with that of your child. If you wanted to be a famous tennis player but didn't make the grade don't expect that your child will want to do the same. Playing a game for enjoyment is one thing; being forced to do so to fulfil dreams of yours is unfair. A child who enjoys a sport may well take it further of his or her own accord when they get older. One who is forced to take on professional practice routines may well begin to hate the sport and rebel against it early.

## PLAYING IN TEAMS

A hatred of team games is something that many people carry with them throughout their lives. The misery of being unable to keep up or not being picked for a team has put them off sport for life.

Primary schools do have team games but not as we remember them. Team games are only introduced to older children in the primary school after they have got used to games of all kinds. Usually the sequence is:

1. individual work

2. working with a partner

3. playing in a small group

4. games in a larger group.

By starting games as individuals and then gradually getting used to working with first a partner and then larger groups or teams children gradually get an increased awareness of rules. Teachers will make sure that children have mastered basic sports skills before introducing them to the concept of rules and team games.

Even when team games are introduced teachers will ensure that the teams are changed frequently; that everyone gets a chance to play in different positions; that teamwork not individual prowess is encouraged; that team games are fun for everyone.

## Learning games skills

All sport, whether played as individuals or in teams means learning some basic physical skills. For example, some Key Stage 1 (5–7) skills include:

- travelling – running, dodging, jumping

- travelling with a piece of equipment – dribbling, carrying

- sending away – passing, throwing, catching

- receiving – stopping, catching, trapping

- poise and control in dance.

For Key Stage 2 (8-11) other skills to be learnt might include:

- net-type games

- fielding-type situations

- invading territory-type games

- different ways of utilising gymnastics skills

- changing speed, shape, direction

- different dance forms

- basic athletic techniques

- negotiating obstacle courses

- swimming unaided.

Younger children in Key Stage 1 start by learning to play freely and then by using small apparatus such as beanbags, hoops, quoits, skipping ropes and playbats. They also learn:

- footwork – running, hopping, skipping

- space awareness – chasing, dodging, avoiding

- ball skills – sending using hands and feet; hitting, receiving and travelling with a ball

- games skills – playing alone or with a partner using simple rules.

In Key Stage 2 your child will learn to increase his or her skills at sending, receiving and travelling with a ball. They will also learn new skills such as:

- bouncing a ball by patting and moving along

- aiming bean bags or balls at markers or hoops

- further sports skills such as jumping and landing correctly

- small-sided and simplified versions of recognised team and individual games

- climbing skills.

## Helping your child with sport

You can have a lot of fun helping your child improve his or her sport skills whether you yourself are good at sport or not. It's a great way to enjoy being with your child and to keep fit and have fun at the same time.

Most parents know how much enjoyment children can get from kicking a ball around or throwing a frisbee, but why not try these ideas too:

- Put up a netball/basketball net in your yard or garden if possible.

- Put some markers down in the park and ask your child to dribble between them.

- Get some short handled bats (usually plastic) with a light ball or shuttlecock so that you and your child can play hitting games.

- Find a wall and give your child a piece of chalk -let them raise their arm above their head and jump as high as they can to make a mark on the wall – can they beat that mark?

*Making a beanbag*

A beanbag is a useful piece of small equipment. If you can't buy one, make your own. Use a piece of closely woven material and sew it to make a bag about 150mm square. Fill it two thirds full with dried lentils or split peas. Fold over the final edge and sew it together with small firm stitches.

## Playing with friends

Even if your child does not want to do any team games he or she will enjoy playing games with friends. For example, you could take a group of your child's friends to the park and keep an eye on them while they play football or running games, skateboards or throw frisbees. If your child is not keen on team activities they can go swimming with friends, play bat and ball games or use climbing equipment together.

## FINDING CLUBS

If your child enjoys games or sport and wants to do more you can look for a club to give them more opportunity to play and more practice. But remember what I said earlier about nor forcing your child to pursue a professional career in sport early. You might find the following kinds of clubs in your area:

- after school clubs

- local sports clubs

- holiday sports clubs

- children's sports clubs

- sports clubs at local leisure centres.

Before you sign on ask the leader whether your child can attend a session to find out whether they enjoy it. If they do, make sure that they will be looked after and not just left to fend for themselves. It will be no fun for your child if they do not get any tuition to help them improve their skills. Before you let your child attend a sports club ask these questions:

- How much does each session cost?

- Will special clothes and equipment be needed or will the club supply it?

- If I have to buy the clothes and equipment how much will it cost?

- Can equipment be hired or borrowed?

- Will I be expected to stay with my child?

- How long will the sessions be?

- How much tuition will my child get?

### Buying clothes and equipment

If you are expected to provide the necessary clothes and equipment for your child you need to be sure that they are really interested. Make sure that your child will be allowed to attend for so many sessions before they need to make a decision about whether to continue. If they do want to after that then you have several choices about getting the clothes and equipment they need:

- buy it new (if you can afford it)

● buy it second hand (ask the club about sources)

● borrow it from the club or a friend

● pay in instalments through a club scheme.

If your child then gives up the sport, you should be able to resell anything in good condition second hand through the club or by advertising in the local paper.

Look for details about sports clubs in:

● the library

● school notice boards

● local papers

● council leaflets

● advertisements.

## QUESTIONS AND ANSWERS

*Can children with physical disabilities take part in sport?*
Yes, children with disabilities can and should take part in sport. Physical disability is no bar to enjoyment – think of the Olympic wheelchair athletes and basketball players. The class teacher will ensure that your child is given every opportunity to participate as much as possible.

*I always hated sport. How can I encourage my child to enjoy it?*
Now is a good time to reassess your attitude to sport! Make the most of the opportunity to take part in new activities with your child. Choose a totally new activity that you and your child can learn together.

Sports centres and leisure centres often run adult beginners classes as well as children's classes. Your child will enjoy sharing an activity with you and will be encouraged by seeing that you have started at the beginning too. You will enjoy learning new skills and sharing the experience with your child.

## CASE STUDIES

### Sally buys Geoff a football
For his birthday Sally buys Geoff a football. But Geoff looks unhappy.

'I haven't got anyone to play with', he says. Sally talks to her friends and arranges to take a group of children to the park on Saturday. She lets them play with Geoff's football but gives them two simple rules: 'No hitting or kicking each other and give everyone a go with the ball'. The children manage the first rule but have trouble with the second. Geoff ends up in tears because he never gets to kick his own ball! Sally decides to organise a simple game involving dribbling the ball and kicking it to the next person. Everyone gets a go – and then an ice-cream! They all say they enjoyed the afternoon a lot and Geoff arranges to play with them again.

## Becky goes to swimming club

Becky not only enjoys swimming but is good at it. She is confident and happy in the water and looks forward to the school swimming lesson every week. 'But it's too short', she says. 'We only get a little time in the pool.' Her parents take her to the local pool on Saturday morning but it is always very crowded. They decide to find Becky a swimming club. After asking around they take her to the 'Penguins' Club at the local pool on Wednesday evening. The leader introduces Becky and gives 20 minutes instruction to her and the other younger children before letting them loose in the pool. A little later he arranges some simple water games. Becky loves it all and is keen to improve enough to get her first badge. Her parents are happy to take her to the pool once a week but stress that she must do other things too.

## Harry watches Mark in a school gym display

Mark has been practising after school for the school gym display. He really prefers football but is good at gym and was chosen to be part of the team. Harry and Eddy go to watch the performance. 'That was very good', says Harry afterwards 'but why weren't you one of the main performers?' 'They do gym better than me', says Mark. He is disappointed that Harry didn't appreciate his efforts and says, 'I don't think I'll try to get in the gym show next year'. Harry realises that Mark had done his best and tries to make up for it. But it is too late. Mark doesn't enjoy gym after that and doesn't try any more.

## SUMMARY

- Try out lots of different sports together.

- Encourage your child to be physically active.

- Don't pressure your child into excessive practice.
- Invite your child's friends to play games.
- Look out for an after school sports club.

# 10

## Reinforcing Social Skills

Learning social skills is just as important as how well a child does at school work. Whatever a child wants to achieve they can do so better if they have the support and co-operation of their peers. **Happy children work better and are more confident in life.**

You can help your child by encouraging them to improve their social skills and by understanding their value to both the child and the school.

### UNDERSTANDING THE IMPORTANCE OF SOCIAL SKILLS

Without good social skills your child will feel isolated and miserable. It will also make it difficult for him or her to cope with life and to concentrate on work.

Learning to get on well with others is an important part of growing up. Some children find it easy; others experience difficulties which could include:

- being shy
- being bullied
- being scared of new situations
- becoming upset with school itself.

*Being shy*
Your child may be shy naturally or because they are unused to being with so many other children. Whatever the reason shyness can be a great handicap.

*Being bullied*
Bullying is a major problem in some schools and even the best run schools have to deal with it occasionally. If your child is being bullied it can be devastating for him or her. If he or she is doing the bullying then it is just as harmful to their development and must be dealt with.

*Being scared of new situations*
Most of us feel nervous when plunged into a new situation with people we don't know. Perhaps your child feels overwhelmed by the business of coping with new people and new situations in school life.

*Becoming upset with school itself*
It is possible that your child might develop a phobia about school itself. It might stem from a trivial incident unnoticed by you or the teacher or it might develop from a major dislike of some aspect of school such as a particular teacher or lesson. Whatever the reason your child might refuse to go to school until you have worked out what the problem is and dealt with it.

## Giving a helping hand

You and the teacher need to work together to help your child integrate into the class and the school and to get used to co-operating with others.

Even if your child seems well adjusted and happy there will be new situations to cope with. And many children experience changes in their friendships that upset or bewilder them. How many times do we hear the cry 'She isn't my best friend any more!'

Your child will watch how you cope with meeting strangers, how you treat your friends and how you deal with life generally. How can you spot when your child might need help?

*Keeping silent*
If your child comes home from school and seems unusually quiet and doesn't want to discuss the school day something might be wrong. Or if he or she does talk but seems to be deliberately avoiding speaking about a particular person or situation then they could be unhappy about it.

*Becoming aggressive*
A typical sign of unhappiness is a child who becomes aggressive towards others when this is out of character. If your child suddenly starts to become aggressive you should ask yourself whether there is something or someone upsetting them at school.

Once you have discovered that something is upsetting them you should talk to your child about it and then to their teacher. Together you will need to work out strategies for dealing with the problem and making your child more confident again in the school.

## SUPPORTING THE SHY CHILD

Shyness can be paralysing. It is not necessarily the new child at school who feels this. Some children become shy as they get older and are faced with new people to deal with. Shyness can cause difficulty in making friends and so increase a child's isolation.

Talk to your child's teacher. He or she will undoubtedly have already noticed your child's reluctance to join in and their loneliness at playtimes. Discuss how you and the teacher can help your child. You could help your child overcome shyness in a number of ways:

● introduce your child to one or two new children

● give your child some simple social skills to deal with a new situation

● help your child learn simple calming exercises

● gradually introduce your child to larger groups.

### Introducing your child to others

Start by inviting a few children that your child knows by sight around to play. Choose a game that everyone can join in and help all the children to participate. Games which involve calling out a name are a good introduction. Make sure you are there all the time as unobtrusively as possible so that you can encourage your child to join in. You could start by helping them say the speaking parts of the game together and then encourage them to try on their own.

### Providing social skills

Shyness can be the result of simply not knowing what to do or say. As the situation continues it becomes even more difficult to join in socially. Unless your child can join in with others a lot of school work is going to be hard for them.

You have an important part to play by giving your child some simple social skills to help them in any new situation. Here are some examples:

1. Start by practising a simple opening conversation with them:

   'Hallo. My name's Jenny. What's your name?'

   'Hallo. My name's Tom.'

   'Where do you live?'

   'I live in Brixton.'

   'I live in Brixton too. Can you show me what to do with this?'

'Yes, here you are.'

'Thank you.'

By practising imaginary situations you give your child confidence.

2. You could practise getting your child to hand you something that you need or joining in a song together.

3. Teach your child to say 'please' and 'thank you' at the appropriate moments. This might seem old-fashioned but does ease the way.

4. Encourage your child to smile when meeting new children. An anxious-looking child will put other children off. Don't forget to set an example and smile too!

## Learning calming exercises

Teach your shy child some simple calming exercises to help them not to get upset in new situations. Common simple exercises are:

- deep breathing
- relaxing parts of the body in turn
- thinking about a favourite calm situation such as a blue sea
- doing simple exercises (before or after school).

## Introducing your child to larger groups

As your child gets better at being with other people in small groups he or she needs to be introduced to larger groups. Your child's teacher may have eased the situation by helping your child to work in small groups in the classroom but the difficulty may still lie with working in large groups such as in PE lessons or whole class learning or going out on school trips.

If the school allows it accompany one or two of the school trips your child goes on. Not only will it reassure your child but it will be a help to the staff to have an extra adult to help them with the class.

At home you could show videos of children working in larger groups or playing together and show your child how the simple social skills you taught them can help.

## DEALING WITH BULLYING

Bullying in schools is not confined to secondary age. It can start early in a child's school life and last for a long time if not stopped. It might involve:

- physical attacks

- verbal cruelty

- continued threats

- racial harassment

- sexual harassment.

All schools should now have an anti-bullying policy and strategies for helping both the victim and the bully. These policies should be made clear to all parents so if you do not know what they are ask the teacher for a copy of the details.

In schools bullying is usually dealt with by:

- stopping it immediately it starts

- giving the victim support and strategies for coping

- re-educating the bully about behaviour

- including bullying as a subject in all class discussions so as to change peer group behaviour and attitudes.

## Finding out if your child has been bullied

Your child might tell you directly that he or she is being bullied. But you might find out by other means. It is important to listen to your child and observe his or her behaviour. Signs of bullying can include:

- becoming withdrawn

- suddenly wanting your company on the way to school

- finding excuses for not going to school

- coming home with excessive bruises or scratches

- frequently coming home with ripped or excessively dirty clothes

- frequently having broken or mislaid possessions

- becoming easily upset

- suddenly having difficulty sleeping

- developing a compulsive habit

- starting to talk to him or herself.

## Helping your child if bullied

If your child is the victim of bullying you need first to be reassuring and then to talk to the school about strategies for dealing with it. It is not necessarily a good idea to withdraw a child from class where bullying takes place because that gives a sense of defeat to your child and enhances the bully's reputation for toughness.

Together you and the teacher must make it clear to your child that they can overcome the problem and that the bully will not be allowed to get away with such behaviour again.

However, many parents do not feel that the school does enough about the bully and that the victim is stigmatised and not given enough help. If you feel this is the case do not hesitate to talk to the child's teacher and if necessary the head teacher. (See Chapter 1 about talking to staff.)

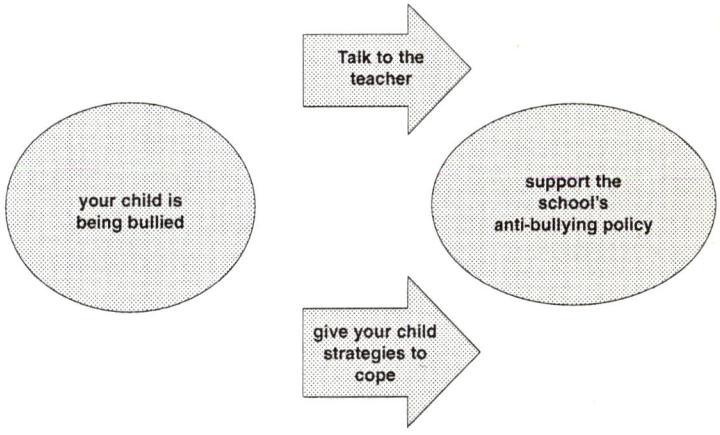

Fig. 10. Dealing with bullying.

*Hitting back*

Do *not* teach your child to hit back however much you feel that it would be appropriate and would stop the bully. If you do you will be condoning inappropriate behaviour and, if caught, your child will have to be punished for fighting. Unfair as it may seem the school cannot allow fighting for whatever reason.

## Finding out whether your child is the bully

If your child is the bully it is distressing but it must be dealt with for the sake of your child and the other children.

Bullies are usually one of two types:

1. A spoilt child.

2. A child who has been bullied who bullies in turn.

Children who bully do so to enjoy power and to feel strong. They need to have their behaviour redirected. You can do this by observing their habits and behaviour and co-operating with the school's anti-bullying strategies. Together you should be able to discourage your child from such antisocial behaviour.

## HELPING YOUR CHILD DEAL WITH NEW SITUATIONS

Your child will be constantly introduced to new situations in their school life. It is important that they can deal with such occasions in a positive manner or else they risk missing out on many important educational experiences. Examples of new situations your child might encounter include:

- eating dinner in a dinner hall

- going on a school trip

- going to assembly

- going swimming

- being in a school play/performance.

These might not seem momentous to us but to some children they can seem frightening. By giving your child strategies for coping with new situations you will be making them more positive and outgoing. By helping your child you will be learning how to cope with situations yourself. Many of us are shy and by helping our own children overcome shyness we become less shy ourselves.

## HELPING YOUR CHILD MAKE FRIENDS

Some children find making friends hard even if they want to. They may be shy or they may inadvertently put other children off. Whatever the reason, being unable to make friends when everyone else seems to manage can be upsetting for any child.

You can help by following the strategies suggested for shy children above. You can also introduce your child to clubs and groups where they have an interest and can join in or quietly watch if they want to. There are groups and clubs for virtually any interest or hobby your child might have. Ask at school or in the local library.

Often groups have special young people's sessions where younger members can meet, watch others and learn about the club's interest.

If you cannot find a group to interest your child locally then look for national groups. These often have a children's or young people's section. They arrange outings and provide newsletters and magazines as well as information and ideas for pursuing the hobby.

Even if your child cannot go to meetings locally there is often an opportunity to find pen friends.

## Finding other ways to make friends

Making friends can stake many forms. These are some ways:

- pen friends
- by e-mail (subject to safety guidelines)
- school clubs
- national clubs
- local clubs
- holiday groups.

Some of these are long distance, but if your child is shy or doesn't make friends easily writing to a penfriend can be a good way to become confident about getting to know someone.

## QUESTIONS AND ANSWERS

*I'm just as shy as my child. How can I help her become more outgoing?*
Both you and your child can practise some of the strategies for involving new people and situations discussed earlier in this chapter. Do things together where you can meet adults while your child plays. At an after school club, for example, smile and say hallo to at least one person. Encourage your child to do the same to another child. You will find that you will have a lot in common with other parents and a topic of conversation – your children. You and your child will give each other confidence. Remember that smiling gets you a long way!

*My child is a bully. Should I punish him?*
Make your disapproval clear to your child but also be supportive of any efforts he makes to improve his behaviour. The best way of changing his behaviour is to ensure that you and he co-operate fully with the school's anti-bullying programme.

*My child won't go to school. What can I do?*
You have a duty to ensure that your child attends school. But there may be a problem that your child has not told you about. Discuss it with your child and the school. If there is a problem, for example bullying, co-operate with the school to get it sorted out. Once your child knows the problem is being dealt with he or she will feel more confident about returning.

## CASE STUDIES

### Sally talks to Geoff's teacher

Sally sometimes helps out in Geoff's class and on school trips. One day she realises Geoff is becoming very withdrawn. He won't tell her what's wrong. She knows that his teacher, Mrs Smith, is very busy during the day so she arranges to meet her after school one day for half an hour. Mrs Smith tells Sally that Geoff seems to be worried about going to assemblies but she can't find out why. When Sally asks Geoff about it he says 'There are too many people'. He is nervous about sitting with so many larger children. Sally tells Mrs Smith, who arranges for Geoff to sit next to her a few times. Gradually he becomes more confident and agrees to sit next to his friends.

### Becky makes new friends

Becky is becoming more confident but still finds it hard to make friends. Her parents decide to help her join a history club because she likes history projects at school. The local archaeology society has a junior group and is held on Saturday afternoon at the local museum. Her mother finds out about it and asks Becky if she would like to go. Becky is excited but worried about meeting new people. Her mother asks the organiser if she can stay too for the first time Becky goes. This is agreed and Becky attends her first meeting. The leader introduces her to other children her age and then takes all the group on a tour of the Roman part of the museum and then upstairs to handle Roman pots and other artefacts. Becky is so interested in it all that she starts chatting happily to the other children. Becky's mother is clearly not needed! The next

Saturday Becky is happy to be left and one of the children comes up to say hallo to her straight away.

## Harry stops Mark bullying

Harry is horrified to be told by Mark's teacher that he has been bullying a younger boy at playtime. When he tackles Mark about it Mark says he 'doesn't know' why he does it. Harry makes Mark understand that he does not approve of such behaviour. He accompanies Mark to a meeting with the teacher to hear what strategies will be set in motion. He tells Mark 'I expect you to do what the school says'. Mark knows that Harry will check with the teacher and begins to improve his behaviour. It doesn't happen immediately but by the end of term his teacher can say 'Mark seems to have given up bullying'.

## SUMMARY

- Remember that social skills are important for children.

- Teach your child strategies to cope with new situations and people.

- If your child is bullied inform the school.

- If your child is the bully co-operate with the school's efforts to change his or her behaviour.

# Glossary

**Attainment targets.** A group of learning skills or facts needed to understand a subject.

**Core curriculum.** A group of subjects followed by all pupils.

**Core subjects.** English, Maths and Science within the National Curriculum.

**Curriculum.** The subjects that pupils must study while they are at school.

**Dyslexia.** A specific learning difficulty resulting in problems with reading and writing.

**IT (Information Technology).** Modern technology enabling communication across the world, for example, computers and videos.

**Key Stage.** The programme of study to be taught leading to a Key Reporting Stage. In primary school the Key Stages are Key Stage One (five to seven years) and Key Stage Two (seven to 11 years).

**Key Reporting Stages.** In primary school these are the ages of seven and 11 when pupils are assessed on attainment targets for those stages.

**National Curriculum.** A basic curriculum for all schools set out in the Education Reform Act 1988.

**Parents' Association.** An association or committee of parents of children at a school. Such associations used to be called Parent Teacher Associations (PTAs) but are now more often called Parents' Associations or Friends of the School.

**PE (Physical Education).** Physical activities such as gymnastics, dance, games and swimming.

**Parent governor.** A parent elected to the governing body of a school. The head teacher is in charge of the daily running of the school but is answerable to the governing body.

**Profiles.** Groups of attainment targets, which are themselves groups of learning skills and facts.

**Programme of study.** The subject matter that is taught at each Key Stage.

**RE (Religious education).** This includes a daily religious act of worship that must be wholly or mostly broadly Christian unless the school has applied to conduct worship broadly of another faith.

**Reading scheme.** A particular set of books used in a specified order used to teach reading.

**SAT (Standard Assessment Task).** Activities designed to find out what level each child is at in National Curriculum subjects.

**Scheme of work.** The plan of work teachers devise for each child to enable them to progress through the National Curriculum levels.

**SEN (Special Educational Needs).** A child is said to have special needs if he or she has a learning difficulty needing special educational provision.

# Further Reading

## BOOKS FOR PARENTS

*A Parents' A–Z of Education*, Hilary Mason and Tony Ramsey (Chambers, 1992).

*Bright Ideas: Language Activities*, Irene Yates (Scholastic, 1990).

*Bullying – A Practical Guide to Coping in Schools*, Michele Elliot (Longman, 1991).

*Children and Technology*, Katrina Blythe (Nash Pollock, 1996).

*Children Solve Problems*, E de Bono (Penguin, 1972).

*Dyslexia: A Parents' Survival Guide*, Christine Ostler (Ammonite, 1991).

*Helping Your Child To Read*, Jonathan Myers (How To Books, 1996).

*Help Your Child with Maths*, ed. Angela Walsh (BBC Books, 1988).

*Governor's Handbook* (ACE,1992).

*Help Your child with Maths*, M R Edwards (CUP, 1991).

*How To Be An Effective School Governor*, Polly Bird (How To Books, 1995).

*Learning in Tandem: involving parents in their children's education*, Ruth Mertenns, Alan Newland and Susie Webb (Scholastic, 1995).

*Reading Together Parents' Handbook*, Myra Bars and Sue Ellis (Walker Books, 1998).

*Teach Your Child How To Think*, E de Bono (Penguin, 1993).

## BOOKS FOR FIVE TO SEVEN YEAR OLDS

*Alfie Gets in First*, Shirley Hughes (Red Fox, 1997).

*Burglar Bill*, Janet and Allan Ahlberg (Mammoth, 1989).

*Dogger*, Shirley Hughes (Random, 1993).

*The Enormous Crocodile*, Roald Dahl (Puffin, 1980).

*Eureka! An Illustrated History of Invention*, E de Bono (Thames and Hudson, 1974).

*How It All Began: The Stories behind Those Famous Names*, Maurice Baren (Smith Seile, 1992).

*I Din Do Nuttin and Other Poems*, John Agard (Magnet, 1984 ).

*I for Invention: Stories about Everyday Inventions*, Meredith Hooper (Pan Macmillan/Piccolo, 1992).

*My Naughty Little Sister*, Dorothy Edwards (Mammoth, 1989).
*Operation Hedgehog*, M Lane (Walker Books, 1991).
*Peabody*, Rosemary Wells (Macmillan, 1984).
*The New Shell Book of Firsts*, Patrick Robinson (Headline, 1995).
*Tales for Telling*, Leila Berg (Methuen, 1983).
*Teddybears One to Ten*, S Gretz (Collins, 1986).
*The Trouble with Dad*, B Cole (Mammoth, 1995).

## BOOKS FOR EIGHT TO ELEVEN YEAR OLDS

*Charlotte's Web*, E B White (Puffin, 1993).
*Clever Polly and the Stupid Wolf*, Catherine Storr (Puffin, 1995).
*Fungus the Bogeyman*, Raymond Briggs (Puffin, 1990).
*James and the Giant Peach*, Roald Dahl (Puffin, 1996).
*Ten in A Bed*, Allan Ahlberg (Puffin, 1990).
*The Good Tiger*, Elizabeth Bowen (Methuen, 1981).
*The Indian in the Cupboard*, Lynne Reid Banks (Harper Collins, 1995).
*The Iron Man: A Story in Five Nights*, Ted Hughes (Faber, 1994).
*The Lion, The Witch and the Wardrobe*, C S Lewis (Harper Collins, 1998).
*Revolting Rhymes*, Roald Dahl (Puffin, 1984).
*The Very Hungry Caterpillar*, E Carle (Mantra Publications, 1997).
*You Can't Catch Me!*, Michael Rosen (Scholastic, 1996).

# Useful Addresses

Advisory Centre for Education (ACE), 1b Aberdeen Studios, 22 Highbury Grove, London N5. Tel: (0171) 354 8321. (Mon to Fri 2–5pm) Internet – http://www.ace.ed.org.uk.
E-mail: ace-ed@easynet.co.uk.

Attention Deficit Disorder (ADD) Information Service, PO Box 230, Hayes, Middlesex NA8 9HL. Tel: (0181) 905 2031.

Anti Bullying Campaign (ABC), 6 Borough High Street, London SE1 9QQ. Tel: (0171) 378 1446. Fax: (0171) 348 8374.

British Dyslexia Association (BDA), 98 London Road, Reading RG1 5AU. Helpline: (0118) 966 8271. Fax: (0118) 935 1927.
E-mail (helpline): info@dyslexiahelp-bda.demon.co.uk.

Department for Education and Employment (DfEE), Sanctuary Buildings, Great Smith Street, London SW1P 3BT. Tel: (0171) 925 5000. Fax: (0171) 925 6000.
E-mail: info@dfee.gov.uk.

The DfEE Publications Centre, PO Box 5000, Sudbury, Suffolk CO10 6YJ.

Health Education Authority, Hamilton House, Mabledon Place, London WC1H 9TX. Tel: (0171) 383 3833. Fax: (0171) 0387 0550.

The National Association for Gifted Children (NAGC), Elder House, Milton Keynes MK1 1LR. Tel: (01908) 673 677.
E-mail: mailto:nagc@rmplc.co.uk.
Internet – http://www.rmplc.co.uk/orgs/nagc/index.html.

The National Association for Primary Education (NAPE), University of Leicester, Queens Building, Barrack Road, Northampton NN2 6AF. Tel: 01604-636326. Fax: 01604-636328.
E-mail: nationaloffice@nape.org.uk.
Internet – http://www.nape.org.uk.

National Association of Governors and Manageres (NAGM), Suite 36/38, 21 Bennetts Hill, Birmingham B2 5QP. Tel: (0121) 643 5787.

National Confederation of Parent Teacher Associations, 2 Ebbsfleet Industrial Estate, Stonebridge Road, Northfleet, Gravesend, Kent DA11 9DZ. Tel: (01474) 560681.
Internet – http://www.rmplc.co.org.uk/orgs/ncpta.

The Sports Council, Information Centre, 16 Upper Woburn Place, London WC1H 0QP. Tel: (0171) 388 1277 (9am–12.30pm, 1.30–5pm Mon to Fri). Fax: (0171) 383 5740.

# Index

LIBRARY
RUGBY COLLEGE

## HELPING YOUR CHILD TO READ
### How to prepare the child of today for the world of tomorrow

**Jonathan Myers**

In our fast moving, computerised world, reading is absolutely vital. It is the key basic skill that children and adults need to transmit information. And reading is fun too. With its lively text, examples and case studies, this forward looking book shows how easy it is for you to get your child on the right road to reading success. Jonathan Myers BSc PGCE is an educational consultant.

*141pp. illus. 1 85703 192 X.*

## PARENTING PRE-SCHOOL CHILDREN
### How to cope with common behavioural problems

**Paul Stallard**

Being a parent is undoubtedly the most responsible and demanding job people ever do – yet there is no training. This book provides parents and childcare professionals with clear ideas about how good behaviour can be encouraged, plus step-by-step guidance on how difficulties can be resolved. Paul Stallard is a Chartered Clinical Psychologist with two young children of his own. He works in the Health Service helping parents to find effective ways of dealing with their children's difficulties.

*144pp. illus. 1 85703 266 7.*

## RAISING THE SUCCESSFUL CHILD
### How to encourage your child on the road to emotional and learning competence

**Sylvia Clare**

Success comes in many shapes and forms, and goals imposed from external sources, even from a beloved parent, have limited intrinsic values to the child. The more a child is freed from external expectations, the more likely he or she is to succeed within his or her own terms of reference. This book includes three children's stories, to be read aloud, which will allow the child to interpret his or her world, understand how to face difficult situations and how to address learning opportunities. Sylvia Clare has 16 years' experience as a teacher of psychology and child development. She is also a parent, foster parent and therapist.

*144pp. illus. 1 85703 353 1.*

LIBRARY
RUGBY COLLEGE